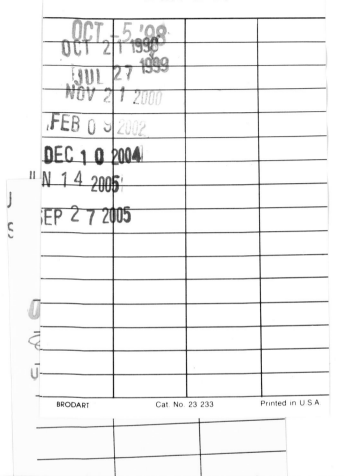
3908

Wallace, Garth, 1946-
  Don't call me a legend : the extraordinary story of
international pilot Charlie Vaughn / by Garth Wallace.
--Merrickville, Ont. : Happy Landings, [1996]
  234 p., [8] p. of plates : ill., ports. ; 24 cm.

826290   ISBN:0969732236

1. Vaughn, Charlie. 2. Air pilots - Canada -
Biography. 3. Airplanes - Ferrying. I. Title

43   98AUG27   3559/ex   1-530167

Other books by Garth Wallace
published by Happy Landings

FLY YELLOW SIDE UP
- Humorous bush flying stories

PIE IN THE SKY
- Fun tales of a small town flying school

BLUE COLLAR PILOTS
- A tongue-in-cheek tribute to the real pilots in aviation

DON'T CALL ME A LEGEND

The extraordinary story of international pilot
Charlie Vaughn

all the best,
Garth *Charlie*

by Garth Wallace

Published by

Happy Landings

Canadian Cataloguing in Publication Data

DON'T CALL ME A LEGEND

The extraordinary story of international pilot Charlie Vaughn

Wallace, Garth, 1946 -

ISBN 0-9697322-3-6

1. Charlie Vaughn. 2. Air pilots - Canada - Biography.
3. Airplanes - Ferrying. I. Title.

TL540.V38W34 1996   629.13'092   C96-900853-8

Edited by: Sari Funston
            Liz Wallace

Typesetting
and proof-reading: Ohlmann Editorial and Design

Cover layout and printing: Tri-Graphic, Ottawa

Written, typeset, printed and bound in Canada.

Published by: Happy Landings
                RR # 4,
                Merrickville, Ontario
                K0G 1N0

        and   812 Proctor Ave.
                Ogdensburg, New York
                13669

                Tel.: 613-269-2552

This book is dedicated to anyone who wants to be a pilot — go for it!

DON'T CALL ME A LEGEND

CONTENTS

Chapter One - The Passion

Chapter Two - Finally Flying

Chapter Three - Webster Trophy

Chapter Four - Ag-Flying

Chapter Five - Homebuilding

Chapter Six - Charter Flying

Chapter Seven - More Charter

Chapter Eight - First Ferry

Chapter Nine - Floatplane Flying

Chapter Ten - Air Racing

Chapter Eleven - Black September

Chapter Twelve - Seaplane Racing

Chapter Thirteen - Helicopter

Chapter Fourteen - Variety

Chapter Fifteen - Ferrying

Chapter Sixteen - Hawaii

Chapter Seventeen - Wes McIntosh

Chapter Eighteen - Buffalos to the Middle East

Chapter Nineteen - Around the World

Chapter Twenty - Ghana again and again and again

Chapter Twenty-one - Test Pilot

Chapter Twenty-two - Sri Lanka

Chapter Twenty-three - From Brussels or bust

Chapter Twenty-four - Hatchet job

Chapter Twenty-five - Italy was supposed to arrange it

Chapter Twenty-six - Rather fly than eat

Chapter Twenty-seven - The Crash

Chapter Twenty-eight - Papua, New Guinea

Chapter Twenty-nine - Thailand

Chapter Thirty - Owen Mcdougall

Chapter Thirty-one - Botswana

Chapter Thirty-two - Simon says

Chapter Thirty-three - Mcdougall again

Chapter Thirty-four - Grecian heat

Chapter Thirty-five - Bad Attitude to Africa

Chapter Thirty-six - To Russia with money

Chapter Thirty-seven - To Russia with perfume

Chapter Thirty-eight - Don't Call me a Legend

Preface

Don't Call Me a Legend is based on interviews with Charlie Vaughn and some of the pilots who shared a cockpit with him. Any misrepresentation of persons, places or events is strictly unintentional.

Garth Wallace
Ottawa, 1996

CHAPTER ONE

1926 - 1945 - The Passion

Charlie Vaughn's love of airplanes was advertised by the sight of him chasing free-flight models around the neighbourhood.

Charlie Vaughn was born in St. Catharines, Ontario, on October 1, 1926. He grew up on the 70-acre family farm in the house next door to where he lives today. Then, the farm was a combination vineyard and dairy operation. His dad hired help during the 1930s, but Charlie and his older brother Bill did chores every morning before going to school and every night.

At a young age Charlie developed a fierce enthusiasm for airplanes that can be understood only by adventure-starved, mechanically-minded boys growing up in the depression. This passion for aviation was ignited by a family friend in Toronto named Earnshaw who built a biplane in his garage. Airplanes were a relatively rare sight in those days. The young Vaughn was fascinated by them. Charlie never got a ride in Earnshaw's biplane, but just seeing it fired his imagination. He built model airplanes and flew them over the cow pasture at home.

I saved pennies for months, Charlie recalls, and bought a gas-powered, free-flight model airplane from Jack Dunham's hobby shop in St. Catharines. It was one of those stick fuselage models with a large, poly-dihedral wing. There were no glow plugs in those days, Charlie recalls with a laugh. The tiny engine had external points, coil and condenser and required several nipped fingers to start. I tried to set the rudder so the airplane would stay in a free-flight circle, but it never did.

Charlie's love of airplanes, advertised by the sight of him chasing the model around the neighbourhood, led to his first airplane ride. Bill Drury, son of a family living near the Vaughn farm, was a civilian pilot who flew in the bush until the beginning of World War II. Drury became an instructor and head of the No. 9 Elementary Flying Training School in St. Catharines. He promised the thirteen-year-old an airplane ride in the Spring of 1940. All Charlie had to do was get to the airport on the other side of town. He couldn't walk the eight kilometres each way because there wasn't enough time. The war had taken the hired men from the farm. Charlie and his brother were doing double duty at home. Airplane rides didn't qualify for time off.

My dad was a hard man. He believed if you were on the farm, you worked. I discovered that a nearby pig farm was hauling garbage from the kitchens at the new military airport. I hitched a ride on the garbage truck while my brother covered for me by working extra hard in the barn. It wouldn't be the last time Bill did that.

Construction had turned the airport into a sea of mud. Nothing had been paved yet. It was difficult for them to pull the airplane out of the hangar with a tractor. I thought we wouldn't go up.

They did. The airplane was a Fleet Finch, a 90-horse, Kinner-powered open cockpit biplane, made in Ft. Erie, Ontario, not far from St. Catharines.

Drury roared through the mud with full power. We barely accelerated at all, but somehow he forced the little airplane into the air. He flew aerobatics during the entire short flight. My knees were shaking uncontrollably the whole time, but it wasn't because I was scared. I loved every minute of it. I was shaking from excitement.

Drury cut a dashing figure in his crisp commandant's uniform. He became an instant hero to Charlie. The youngster was hooked. He wanted to be a pilot. But there would be no more flying for the farmbound enthusiast during the war. In 1941, Charlie finished high school and farmed full-time. It was hard work.

It still is.

When Charlie was old enough to enlist, the British Commonwealth Air Training Plan was in high gear in Canada. Every able-bodied young man with his eye on the sky was being trained as a pilot, but not Charlie. He was given a farm deferment. In the Vaughn family there was no question of either of the boys joining the air force or anything else. Their war effort would be working the land. Charlie would stay on the farm and that was that. A more maverick personality might have left anyway, but the young Vaughn drew heavily on a large capacity for patience. He stayed home and worked the farm.

There was plenty of air activity over Niagara to remind Charlie that he would rather fly than milk cows. Within 30 miles of his house there were military flying training schools at St. Catharines, Niagara Falls, Welland, Dunnville, Hamilton, Cayuga, Jarvis and Hagersville. But there was no civilian flying training available. It had been suspended in favour of the war effort.

Bill Drury left the St. Catharines E.F.T.S. to join the coastal patrol in Halifax. He died in 1943 from an untreated case of chicken pox. It would be five years before Charlie would get another ride in an airplane.

CHAPTER TWO

1945 - 1951 - Finally flying

"I'm not afraid Charlie, you can go faster now."
Maude Vaughn, Charlie's mother

At the end of the war, Charlie was about to turn nineteen-years-old. He and his brother Bill had finished high school and were working on the farm full-time. They milked 40 head and worked 160 acres of mixed pasture and grapes.

On September 16, 1945, Charlie hitchhiked 20 miles to Warren Air Service in Hamilton, Ontario. Charlie Warren had opened the first civilian flying school in the area at the old Barton Street airport in the east end of town.

If I had taken the bus, I wouldn't have had enough money to fly. The lessons were $10 an hour dual and $8 solo. At the time my dad was paying me $40 a month.

Each lesson required that I get ahead of the farm chores, hitch a ride to Hamilton, fly, and then hurry back to make up for the lost time. I didn't get to hang around like other students. There was too much work on the farm.

Charlie did get some help creating flying time from Ralph Lockey who farmed across the road. Lockey had learned to fly with Tom Williams before the war. He understood Charlie's ambition to become a pilot and helped Bill Vaughn Jr. with Charlie's chores when he was gone.

Charlie flew Canadian-built 65-horsepower Piper J-3 Cubs. A young entrepreneur named Glenn White was assembling them under licence from Piper at his Cub Aircraft Company in Hamilton.

They were the most basic airplanes I have ever flown. They didn't have radios, electrics or much heat. One had a tail skid instead of brakes. The few instruments and all the heat were blocked by the flying instructor who sat in the front seat. I remember that the airspeed indicator was a little plate on a spring attached on a wing strut outside. The air pushed it back as the speed increased. The instructor rarely spoke because it required him to turn and yell over his shoulder. I couldn't hear half of what he said. I learned more about flying from talking to the other pilots on the ground than I did from the instructor.

Charlie took half hour lessons; it was all he could afford. He didn't mind because it was too cold to stay up longer. It took him all winter of 1945-46 to accumulate six hours.

For his first solo, the instructor flew with Charlie for one circuit and then asked him if he thought he could take it around on his own. The shy farmer said, "I think so." The instructor told him that wasn't good enough and they had to go around again.

I spoke right up when he asked me again after the next landing and said, "I know I can, I know I can." He let me go.

After Charlie's solo, his instructor, Nick Seldon, became chief instructor of a flying club opening in Welland, Ontario, eight miles south of the Vaughn farm. Charlie followed him to the new school.

They had two new Aeronca Champions at Welland. I thought I was really stepping up in the world. The student pilot sat in the front seat. The Champs had real heaters, real instruments and tremendous visibility. I didn't believe they could make airplanes any better than that.

Charlie's dad's only concession to the young Vaughn's passion for flying was to allow him to use the farm truck to drive to the Welland Airport, but it took another year of half-hour lessons before Charlie took his flight test. He had accumulated 8:25 dual and 10:30 solo.

It wasn't really a case of being ready for the flight test. Nick just said one day that the inspector was going to be there that week and he thought I should take a shot at it. For the test, a Department of Transport inspector sat in his car parked beside the runway and watched. I had to do three circuits with a power off approach on each and a dead stick landing that resulted in the aircraft stopping within 100 feet of the car. The inspector rolled his window down so he could hear if I cheated with a little power. Then I had to climb to 3,000 feet, fly a couple of figure eights, spin, recover, and then do a forced approach to the car.

Charlie passed and received a Certificate of Proficiency for Flying Machines. It was June 10, 1947.

When asked what drove him to spend his piti-fully small amount of spare money and spare time over two years to receive a pilot licence, Charlie just shrugs. To a Depression-raised farm boy, it was not an un-usual accomplishment.

His next goal was to build flying time to carry passengers. In those days 25 hours of solo experience was required before flying with passengers.

Charlie rented aircraft at the Niagara District Airport in St. Catharines where he had taken his first airplane ride. Morley Gain had started Aero Services. Alec Marshall was the chief instructor and Doug Stewart was the instructor who checked him out. Aero Services had Piper J-3s, a Fleet Canuck and an Ercoupe. The eager Charlie flew them all. The St. Catharines Flying Club also restarted operations on the same field. Charlie flew their Tiger Moth. Seven years after his first airplane ride, Charlie was finally flying the same skies that he could only gaze at during the war. He was living the dream he had held for so long.

At the time, I never thought I would go any further with my flying. I was busy farming. I just flew whenever I could.

Charlie received his first big break in his flying career in 1949. Through a friend of a friend, he met Wally Claire. Claire was an American pilot who operated a Grumman Widgeon for hire from Grand Island, New York, near Niagara Falls. Claire was looking for a co-pilot willing to ride with him just for the experience. He didn't have to ask Charlie twice.

The Widgeon was a huge step from the 65-horsepower, fabric-covered Cubs and Champs. It was an amphibious aircraft, a flying boat with twin, 200-hp Ranger engines.

Wally was not a good teacher, but I learned a lot by watching him and then trying it myself. He introduced me to handling an aircraft on water, radio work, constant speed propellers, multi-engine handling and instrument flying.

Wally let me do most of the flying. He was more interested in reading a book or sleeping. It was great experience for me. I learned to fly in cloud and to follow the old radio ranges. On one passenger charter to Parry Sound, Wally fell asleep while I was flying in cloud. All of a sudden it got very dark and rain started pelting the windshield. Turbulence tossed the Widgeon all over. I had trouble keeping us upright. I had flown right into a thunderstorm. It was like nothing I had ever experienced before. Wally woke up just before we popped out of it. He looked at me with wide eyes and said, "I guess you won't do that again!"

That summer, Charlie added a float rating to his pilot licence. Glen White had taken over Warren Air Service in Hamilton and offered lessons in a J-3 Cub on floats in Burlington Bay.

It was an interesting experience. The 65-hp Cub took forever to get off. It climbed at 60 mph, cruised at 65 and landed at 60. Some days, if there was no wind, we didn't get off at all. If there was a wind, we got off, but when we were flying into it, bicycles passed us on the ground.

In October of 1949, Tom Jones, the Studebaker car dealer in St. Catharines, and a flying buddy of Charlie's, asked him if he would go partners in buying an airplane. Aero Services in St. Catharines couldn't make a go of it and were selling out. They had a Piper L4-B with skis for $1,200.

The thought of owning an airplane was heady stuff for a young man raised in the depression. So was the idea of going into debt. Aero Services agreed to keep the skis and sell the airplane for $1,000. That was it; Charlie borrowed the $500 for his half and they bought the airplane.

The L4-B was the military version of the Piper J-3 Cub. The two models were the same with the addition of more windows on the L4-B. Charlie's airplane had been used during World War II for observation/liaison work. CF-EGJ fills Charlie's pilot log book for the next several pages as he and Jones flew around every chance they could. Owning his own aircraft was one of many things in Charlie's flying career that he had to pinch himself to believe.

Initially the pair kept the L4-B at the Niagara District Airport in St. Catharines, but the hangar rent jumped to $20 a month. Charlie built a T-hangar on the end of the barn, landed on the cow pasture and parked it at home from then on.

The small landing pasture was split halfway across by a set of high voltage hydro transmission lines, but they were no problem. We just landed before them and took off after them. Getting the cows off the runway was more trouble than the wires.

The trusty Cub seldom saw an airport. We kept a drum of gas in the hangar and whenever we went somewhere, we just landed in a convenient field. Tom and I used to fish and duck hunt at Port Rowan on Lake Erie. There was no airport there; we just landed in the field next to the railroad station.

The airplane was a great time builder, although that wasn't my original reason for buying it. I remember a trip Tom and I took to Wiarton where my parents were staying on a holiday. The wind was really strong. It took us four hours and 45 minutes plus a stop in Kitchener for gas. In those days, it was a four-hour drive.

On the way back, we ran into thunderstorms at Mt. Forest. In that airplane you couldn't outrun or circumnavigate thunderstorms, so we landed in a farmer's field. It was pouring rain. The farmer invited us in, dried us off and made tea. When it cleared up, he took down a fence so we could have more room to take off through the mud. We needed it.

Charlie's father mostly ignored his son's flying. Charlie's older brother continued to cover for him if he was delayed on a flight.

The first summer that I parked the airplane on the farm, my mother asked if she could go for a ride. I sat her in the front seat and took off to show her Niagara Falls from the air. As the neighbouring farms slowly slid by underneath, she turned and yelled to me over the roar of the 65 horses straining at full power, "I'm not afraid Charlie; you can go faster now."

CHAPTER THREE

1951 - Webster Trophy competition

"I was just happy to have gone that far."
Charlie Vaughn

$\mathbf{A}$t the time Charlie was taking his first flying lessons in Hamilton he met a pretty young girl at a dance in St. Catharines. Robina McKenzie was a local Bell Telephone operator. Subsequent dates left no doubt in Robina's mind that aviation was already a big part of Charlie's life. "Neither one of us had much money," Robina recalls, "and Charlie spent most of his on flying. One of our dates was a ride in the farm truck to the Hamilton Airport where I watched him take a flying lesson."

The couple were married on April 14, 1951.

After the wedding, Charlie focused on setting goals for his flying activities. He decided to obtain a Commercial Pilot Licence and Instructor's Rating with the L4-B. During 1952, Charlie took lessons with the instructors at the St. Catharines Flying Club. Since he owned his own airplane and had a long love affair with aviation, Charlie's flying ability was better than most pilots his age.

Flying Club instructor Moe Fraser and manager Bob Calendar encouraged Charlie to enter the competition for the Webster Trophy, the supreme award for amateur airmanship in Canada.

Charlie practised with Moe and then flew to Brantford for the Ontario Region Webster Runoffs. Charlie came first and won a berth in the finals. Tom Thususka, an eighteen-year-old from St. Catharines, was second.

At the end of August, Charlie flew to Winnipeg for the national competition in a St. Catharines Flying Club Piper Clipper with Calendar, Thususka and club director Joe Rogers.

The Clipper was bigger and more powerful than my Cub, but not much faster. It took us two days to get there. The engine static was so bad on the Narco Superhomer radio that we had to throttle back and glide every time we used it.

The competition consisted of two flight tests and a cross-country flight judged by Department of Transport inspector Moe Louch and an examiner from the air force. Charlie flew his heart out, scoring 422.54 out of a possible 500. It was good enough for second place, six marks behind Hap Wells. Wells went on to fly for CP Air.

I was just happy to have gone that far.

CHAPTER FOUR

1952 - 1963 - Ag-flying

*"It didn't seem like a week was complete unless I went
to the airport at least once."*

Charlie Vaughn

Charlie's Webster trophy results encouraged him to
consider a full-time aviation career. He had received his
Commercial Pilot Licence just before going to Winnipeg. He
had heard Trans Canada Airlines was hiring pilots, but
competition for the positions was tough. Construction of
Canada's Dewline, a chain of northern radar sites, had just
been completed and flight crews with Douglas DC-3
experience were coming off the job. But Charlie was
encouraged when TCA hired Bob Smallman, a St. Catharines
area pilot. He applied. The reply was brief and unyielding:

Dear Mr. Vaughn:

*Your completed application for employment on Trans-
Canada Airlines flight staff recently received is
acknowledged. As one of our basic requirements for
employment of new pilots involves the age group 18 to
25, I am afraid that this will automatically preclude
you from serious consideration.*

Yours truly,
Garth Edward
Assistant Director
Flight Operations

The letter was dated October 16, 1952. Charlie had turned
twenty-six-years-old two weeks earlier. His first son, Doug,

had been born the week before. It was the airline's loss and general aviation's gain.

St. Catharines Flying Club manager, Bob Calendar needed part-time instructors for weekends. He offered Charlie a job. Charlie agreed and buddied up with Niagara Falls native, Jack Merrett, on the flying instructor course at the club. The two pilots became good friends.

We practised on each other in my L4-B, taking turns as instructor and student. The lesson I recall the most was the spin. Jack acted as the instructor. He demonstrated a spin entry, talking as he went, but he had never spun a Cub before. The airplane flipped over and wound up tight. We were soon pointed straight at the ground and rotating rapidly. Jack suddenly stopped talking and stared at the horizon flipping by the windshield. I think we were only at 3,000 feet to begin with, so I took over control and recovered.

Jack grinned and said, "I knew what to do, but couldn't remember what to say!"

Both pilots finished the course in 1953 and began instructing at the club. Charlie sold the L4-B.

Marty Wolf from near Iroquois Falls, Ontario, had come to St. Catharines from up north to learn to fly. He saw the airplane for sale and agreed to buy it if the price included delivery to his home airport in Porquis Junction near Timmins, Ontario. I accepted his offer.

The route north included a long stretch from Muskoka to Earlton where the only gas was at the air force base in North Bay. I phoned. They told me that airplanes without electrics or radios were not allowed to land there. I rigged a gas tank from an old pick-up truck on the L4-B's turtle deck behind the back seat and ran some copper tubing forward into the nose tank. It wasn't exactly an approved installation, but it worked.

Charlie was over four hours non-stop on the leg to Earlton, including circumnavigating the air base. It was the first of many, much longer, aircraft ferry flights that would come later in his career.

Charlie settled into a routine of farming at home and instructing at the St. Catharines Flying Club in Aeronca Champs, Cessna 140s and a North American Navion.

It didn't seem like a week was complete unless I went to the airport at least once. I got $2 an hour for the flying time. The little extra money was handy, but I had to work long and hard for it.

After instructing for four hours in the Champs on a Sunday, I would be hoarse. To make it through the day, I loosened my seat belt and leaned forward to yell at the students over the engine noise. It worked fairly well, but I remember one lesson where the guy wasn't pushing the stick forward on the stall recovery so I really gave him a blast. It worked too well. On the next stall entry he shoved the stick all the way to the instrument panel. The airplane pitched over into an outside loop, lifting me out of my seat and jamming my head against the ceiling. Then the student froze. I had to cuff him on the back of the head before he would let go of the stick and allow me to recover.

We did night flying instruction on Friday evenings. The theory was that most people could sleep in on Saturday morning. I would milk the cows at 5:00 pm before going out to the airport. We used coal oil lanterns for lights. After filling, cleaning and lighting each one, we loaded them onto a trailer. One guy would drive the tow vehicle and the other would sit on the trailer, dropping the lamps along the edge of the runway. Some nights I might do all that and get thirty minutes of dual circuits before sending a student solo. Then we would pick up the lanterns and go home. I'd get in about 1:30 am and then get up at 5:00 am to milk the cows again.

When Charlie talks about the difficulties in those days, he isn't complaining. It's obvious that he loved the flying or he wouldn't have done it. The instructing led to other types of flying, which was the case with much of his aviation career.

The flying club hosted an airshow every year which gave Charlie the opportunity to see a skydiver for the first time — from above.

I'd seen parachuting before, but not skydiving. At one of the airshows, it was my job to fly a demonstration jumper from France. We removed the door from the Club's Piper PA12, took off and climbed to 5,000 feet over the airport. At the appointed time, I throttled back and slowed down. On the way out the door, the guy caught part of his equipment on the airplane's step and hung there for a moment. He wriggled free and dropped. I watched him go. His parachute didn't open.

From above, a falling body quickly shrinks in size. I thought I had killed the guy because it looked like he must be near the ground when his chute finally did open. I didn't know that the freefall was part of the show.

In 1955, Robina gave birth to their second son, Fred, on March 9. Charlie continued to farm and fly. He was the first pilot in the Niagara area to do aerial frost control with an airplane.

I don't remember where the idea came from, but we knew that on calm, cold mornings in the spring and fall, a temperature inversion often existed close to the ground. A layer of cold air would form next to the ground with warmer air on top. The coldest time of the day is at first light, so I flew over the grapes early in the morning when there was a danger of frost and displaced the warm air down on the crops.

On the cold mornings in May, Charlie would be airborne at 5:00 am in a Piper PA12 rented from the Flying Club to frost fly over his own grapes. He would circle over the farm while working up his nerve to descend into the featureless blackness of "first light". This was his introduction to "agricultural" flying.

Some of the most demanding flying that I have ever done was with Earl Gilks in the pre-dawn darkness of cold spring mornings. I frost flew over our farm while Earl did our neighbour. We flew coordinated overlapping patterns 90 degrees to each other. The concentration required was intense particularly since my pattern was flown under the high-voltage hydro lines running across our property.

Charlie met an ex-air force pilot at a Department of Transport Instructor Refresher Course held in London, Ontario. Merv Hicks had started a crop dusting company in Tillsonburg. The two pilots developed a friendship which led to Charlie flying aircraft for Hicks and Lawrence Ltd. for the next 10 years.

We flew Piper J-3s converted to 85 horsepower. The pilot sat in the front with the hopper installed behind instead of the back seat. A venturi spreader underneath sucked the load out. I started in the spring, fertilizing winter wheat with nitrogen aero prills, and then dusted for insects and mildew.

The dust was so fine it would hang over the fields like a fog. If there was any breeze, we had to start across the downwind side of the field and work upwind in order to see. Brights Winery near Niagara Falls owned vineyards so large that we dusted them with three Cubs flying in formation. We put on a real show. The flying was low, usually with the wheels placed between the rows to get the dust under the leaves. The flagmen had to duck every time we flew over.

In those days, people were not as aware of the hazards of chemicals. I always wore a crash helmet but no breathing gear. I remember we dusted the local Boy Scout camp every year with DDT as a public service. They thought it was great. When we flew over, all the kids would rush out to watch. They were entertained and got rid of the mosquitoes at the same time.

One year the Ontario Water Resource Commission hired Hicks and Lawrence to spread a toxic granular substance on the surface of Lake Erie. It was an experiment to kill the algae growing off the Crystal Beach tourist area. The chemical was so dangerous that the loaders were dressed in overall protective clothing. They gave me a mask to wear, but we knew little about the chemicals we were flying. The only part of the job that I considered risky was flying over water in a single-engine airplane.

The public was less sensitive to our work in those days. I did Wally Secord's potatoes every year. Wally was an old holdout on a farm in the middle of the city of St. Catharines. The area around the farm was all residential. I dusted the whole thing. I warned the local police every time I was going to do it. If they received complaints, they never told me about them. You wouldn't get away with that today.

On March 19, 1958, Charlie's third son, Dennis, was born. Charlie continued instructing and crop dusting part time while farming full-time.

The work involved early mornings and late evenings. The low flying required intense concentration, but I enjoyed the challenge.

We put up to eight bags or 400 pounds of dust in the 85-hp Cubs, about double what it was designed to carry. Some of the other ag pilots would start with a full load and stagger off. I always started light and worked up to a comfortable load. Sometimes we'd use my farm strip, but I had a pair of wooden construction barricades that we set up on the concession roads nearby if we needed a longer run on a warm day.

The Brights farms were near the St. Catharines Airport. One day I was there loading dust and met Moe Louch, the Department of Transport inspector who had flown with me during the Webster Trophy competition. I added bags of chemical while we talked, but I stopped at the legal load limit for the Cub. After a while Moe excused himself from the group and said he had to go, "so Charlie can finish loading the Cub!"

Charlie earned a reputation for reliability that followed him through his aviation career, but the flying was not without incident.

I remember Brights had two similar fields, one concession apart from each other. One morning I was leading a formation of three Cubs. The other guys were relying on me to know the area, but I was thinking of the one field while flying the other. The one I was thinking about didn't have any wires. Fortunately the airplanes had cutters protecting the windshield and landing gear. We clobbered a set of wires, but we cut through them before we knew it.

Charlie flew for Hicks for 10 years, switching to Piper Super Cubs in the 1960s. The only other problem he encountered was not his fault, but was nearly his undoing.

A young pilot delivered a Super Cub from St. Thomas to St. Catharines for me to use at Brights. Before departing St. Thomas, he discovered a cap missing from one of the gas tanks and replaced it with an unvented oil cap off Merv's Harvard. He flew here on the other tank. When I loaded up, I naturally switched to the full side. Instead of quitting right away, the engine sucked the aluminum tank slowly in until it had almost completely collapsed. I was just pulling over the wires at the end of a run when the engine stopped. It was not a good spot.

I had conditioned myself to automatically switch fuel tanks whenever I had an engine problem. It worked. In the few seconds I had before ploughing into the vineyard, the engine restarted itself. When I got back to the airport, I climbed up and looked at the wing tank. It was crushed where the tank had collapsed. I couldn't believe the engine suction would have that much force.

Charlie was the only pilot in the area to fly on a pollination program.

St. Catharines Flying Club member Garth Glass owned a pear orchard not far from our place. He wanted to dust his trees with pear pollen from the air and asked me to fly. He purchased the pollen from the United States. It was really expensive so he mixed it with lycopodium powder as a carrier and built a home made hopper-style metering device that was designed to sit between the front and back seats of an aircraft with a nozzle out the door.

I rented a Champ from the Flying Club. Garth installed the spreader and sat in the back seat to operate it. Approaching the orchard, I could see there were wires running along the road. I flew over those and dropped onto the trees. Everything went well until I flew between the house and the barn. I never saw the hydro wire running across there. Its poles were hidden in the trees. We clipped it with the prop and it snagged on the landing gear. There was a loud bang and the airplane immediately started pitching into the orchard. I hit full power and pulled up. The airplane hesitated for a second like it was trying to make up its mind to respond or crash. At the last second, the descent was checked and we staggered away from the trees. We both looked back in time to see the hydro poles on either side go down. Somehow the airplane stayed in the air. We flew back to the airport trailing a long piece of wire.

The experiment cost me the price of a new prop and a cowling repair. We were lucky, but Garth claimed the pollen improved his yield. The next year he bought his own Piper J-3, nicknamed the "Bumblebee," and we used that.

In 1963, Charlie's mom died. She wasn't the only friend Charlie lost that year.

Hicks and Lawrence pilots often stayed at our house when they were working the Niagara area. That was how I came to know Johnny Van Rietveld quite well. Johnny was one of Hicks' most experienced pilots. In 1963 he was rebounding from his first marriage and planning his second. One day he was flying a 450-hp Boeing Stearman biplane out of Hamilton. On his way back to the airport, he ran the airplane out of gas. Deadsticking a Stearman into a field is not easy, but I would have expected someone like Johnny to do it every time. He forgot to close the throttle and as he made his approach, the engine gave him a momentary burst of power.

It was just enough to make him miss the field. He clipped a tree, flipped over and was killed.

After I heard about it, I flew over the wreck. Seeing the crumpled biplane made me realize that if Johnny could run into something he couldn't handle, then there was a lot out there that could catch me.

Charlie had a wife and three boys at home to consider. The incident made him think about other types of flying. He didn't quit crop dusting right away. It has never been Charlie's style to suddenly drop customers and employers, but he gradually withdrew from agricultural flying over the next few years.

The best thing to happen to Charlie in 1963, occurred on the farm. He and Bill Jr. talked their dad into selling the cows and concentrating on grape production.

To this day, I usually wake up at five in the morning. It comes in handy for early departures on a flight, but the rest of the time I still curse those cows.

CHAPTER FIVE

1963 - Homebuilding

"I remember taxiing the fuselage around the yard with my boys in the front seat while we were waiting for the wings to be completed."

Charlie Vaughn

Charlie had always been the most mechanically-minded Vaughn. He started by repairing the family farm machinery and progressed all the way to engine rebuilding. He supplemented his learning-by-doing with local high school courses such as welding. His machine repair reputation spread and he frequently did work for neighbouring farmers.

In 1963, a Rearwin Sportster, a Kinner-powered antique was damaged in a wind storm at St. Catharines. A mechanic from Hamilton was contracted to fix it. He heard that Charlie did some welding and asked him if he could fix the aircraft's bent struts and ferry it to Hamilton.

It was a chance to fly a 1930s aircraft, so I said, "Yes." I welded splices into the struts and re-rigged the airplane. On the way to Hamilton, the engine quit right after takeoff. Before I could do anything, it restarted and ran fine. Against my better judgement, I continued on. I knew if I turned back to St. Catharines, I would probably not get to fly it again.

Charlie has never held aircraft maintenance engineering licences, but the mechanical knowledge he developed in those early days has helped him ferry aircraft around the world. The Hamilton mechanic signed off Charlie's work on the Sportster as soon as he saw it. Word got around that Charlie had mastered the delicate art of gas welding the thin-walled tubing used on aircraft.

I did a lot of work on Bell 47s for Earl Jonz, the mechanic at Niagara Helicopters. The combination of high-cycle sightseeing flights and student pilot training was hard on the airframes.

The welding experience led to my involvement with an aircraft homebuilding project. Ten of us from the flying club decided that a homebuilt aircraft would provide us with some cheap flying. We picked a Pietenpol, a two-place, open cockpit design that had originally been powered by a Ford Model A engine. A group of us built the fuselage in my basement while another group did the wings somewhere else. It was basically a wood and fabric airplane, but I welded all the metal brackets and fittings. We installed a 65-hp Continental aircraft engine instead of a Ford. The Continental was considerably lighter. To rebalance the aircraft, we suspended the fuselage from a barn beam at the aircraft's centre of lift. Then we moved the engine forward until we had the balance right.

I remember taxiing the fuselage around the yard with my boys in the front seat while we were waiting for the wings to be completed. It took the group two and a half years to finish the project. As the most experienced pilot, I was elected to test fly it. We assembled it at the airport in St. Catharines. I decided I needed a parachute even though I didn't know how to jump. But the airplane was small and there was no room for it. I finally found an old military chest pack. I could just fit in wearing it. I was glad I never had to jump.

Charlie installed a g-meter in the airplane and pulled up to 4gs during dive recoveries. The initial spins tended to be flat requiring power for prompt recovery. The barnyard engineers corrected that tendency by adjusting the stabilizer's angle of incidence.

The group flew the Pietenpol for many years.

CHAPTER SIX

1964 - 1967 - Charter

"At that time I would fly anywhere with anybody in anything. I made a little money, but I spent some too. The real reason that I flew was the enjoyment."
                                                    Charlie Vaughn

In 1964, I started charter flying for Commander Aviation in Toronto. Today, a co-pilot must be endorsed on the aircraft he is flying, so he comes to the job qualified with the minimum time and no practical experience. In the 1960s, I worked as a co-pilot with Moe Fraser and Cole McKay on an Aero Commander 500 and a 680FL. I learned something every time I flew with those guys. When I started, I didn't have a Multi-Engine Rating or an Instrument Rating. I learned how to use weather radar, how to avoid icing conditions and thunderstorms, and how to fly in and out of high density areas. I was lucky to gain all that experience without the responsibility of being qualified on the airplanes.

Moe was one of those natural pilots who could be busy running the airplane through a pre-flight check while I was copying a complicated IFR clearance to New York City. If I messed up reading it back, Moe would take over the radio and do it perfectly out of his head.

In that same year, Charlie became the personal pilot of John Rigby. Rigby was the hard-driving but kindly owner of Ontario Construction, a St. Catharines-based company that erected commercial buildings around the province. Rigby owned a single-engine Cessna 182 Skylane. He asked Charlie to fly him in it — everywhere.

By the end of 1964, Charlie was determined to get his Instrument Rating. He did it in typical Vaughn fashion.

Raising three kids on a farm did not leave extra money for flying lessons so Charlie tapped a deep well of airline pilot friends to learn what he needed to know for the instrument tests.

He started in a war surplus Link Trainer at Millardair's hangar in Toronto with Trans Canada Airlines pilot Tom Thususka. John Rigby allowed Charlie to use the Skylane for the flight training. He flew with every St. Catharines-area TCA pilot he knew: Thususka, Jack Smith and Earl Gilks.

On April 26, 1966, 15 months after he had started, Charlie took his IFR flight test in Rigby's Skylane at Toronto International Airport.

The inspector was Harry Kelly. I remember him, not so much for the flight test, but for what happened after. He met me at the Esso corporate aviation lounge at the north end of the field. I was extremely nervous. It was like all my training and experience had left me and I knew nothing. We went flying and maybe I did all right, but I didn't really have any idea. The inspector didn't say much.

When we came back, a red hot lineman was waiting for us. He started tearing a strip off Kelly before the man had a chance to tell me whether I had passed. Kelly had parked and locked his car in the driveway beside the lounge. It was blocking access to the ramp. With the linecrew still chewing him out, Kelly walked over and discovered that he had locked his keys in the car.

I saved his day by using a coat hanger to open the door. He thanked me and said, "Well I guess I have to pass you now."

A pass is a pass. I took it.

That year, Commander Aviation acquired an Aero Commander 680 FLP, a pressurized, top-of-the-line piston-engined corporate airplane. Charlie flew it with Don Morrison who went on to become a Canadair test pilot on the Challenger corporate jet program.

In 1966, Charlie also started flying a corporate Beechcraft Model 18 with Jack Harcourt. The airplane was owned by

Anthes Imperial, a St. Catharines furnace manufacturer. CF-ANT had been the personal transport of Olive Beech, wife of the owner of Beech Aircraft. By 1966, the round-engined Model 18 was too slow for most businesses, but this cream puff corporate airplane was well suited for Anthes' short haul flights.

In the 1960s, Instrument Ratings were valid for six months. When Charlie flew Rigby's Skylane to Toronto International for a renewal flight test, the inspector assigned was Wes McIntosh.

The two men hit it off well together even though they came from different aviation backgrounds. McIntosh was a former Canadian military pilot. He was easy going like Charlie. He liked to talk and Charlie liked to listen. They both loved the challenge of flying well. They quickly developed a mutual respect for each other. Charlie found himself booked with McIntosh every time he scheduled an IFR renewal flight. They became good friends and were destined to fly to all corners of the earth together.

All this time, Charlie was still instructing at the St. Catharines Flying Club on Sundays. This was unique. In those days, flying instructors were either young guys just starting their aviation careers or full-time flying school managers. The youngsters usually lasted a year or two before moving on to less demanding and better paying flying jobs. The managers only flew when they had to.

Long-term part-time instructors were few. They were underpaid and overworked as fill-ins for the regular staff. They were doomed to fly with students they didn't know, giving lessons the other instructors didn't want. For his effort, the part-time instructor in the mid-1960s would be paid $2 an hour for his time in the air. A typical Sunday of instructing at the Club would net Charlie five to ten dollars.

He loved it. Charlie enjoyed flying. He liked people. He also had the experience to teach student pilots a thing or two that the younger, full-time instructors could not. The Department of Transport recognized Charlie's instructing experience by granting him Designated Flight Test Examiner status for Private Pilot candidates, a privilege not given often to part-time instructors.

Charlie gave lessons at the St. Catharines Flying Club most Sundays for 20 years.

CHAPTER SEVEN

1967 - I'll never forget that one

"I decided that he must know something about penetrating thunderstorms that I didn't."

Charlie Vaughn

In January 1967, Charlie started his own training toward a Multi-engine Rating in a rented Piper Apache. He had been flying in twin-engined aircraft off and on for 15 years, but not as pilot-in-command. Charlie had never taken multi-engine training.

The lessons consisted mainly of handling the airplane with one engine throttled back to simulate a failure. The performance of the pudgy, low-powered Apache was underwhelming with both engines running. Level flight with only one powerplant was nearly impossible. Charlie learned to get the most from the Apache in a couple of lessons and passed a multi-engine flight test with DOT inspector Bruce Carter.

Charlie continued training in the Apache for an Instrument Rating on multi-engine aircraft flying with the same friends who had provided his initial instrument instruction. In March, he passed his Multi-Engine Instrument Rating flight test with inspector Wes Mcintosh.

The new qualifications landed Charlie work immediately with Don Whilhelm on a Cessna 411 out of Welland, Ontario, and with Peninsula Air Service in Hamilton. Peninsula was home to Trans Aircraft, Canadian distributor for Piper Aircraft. Charlie flew charters in new six-passenger Piper Aztecs with local pilots Hans Grob, Ross Hannigan, John Galashan and Allan Frosst. Notable passengers included Frank Sherman, head of Hamilton steel giant Dofasco and

Doug Hatch, president of Brights Wines in Niagara Falls. The Brights connection would become especially important later.

Charlie remembers a trip with Allan Frosst that he would like to forget. Like Charlie, Frosst was a part-time pilot who worked "on call". His day job was teaching at McMaster University. Frosst also wrote a column for an aviation magazine.

We were flying an Aztec. Frosst was acting as the captain and I was working the radios as the co-pilot. We headed south into the United States. A thunderstorm blocked our path.

"Ask the centre for lower for thunderstorm penetration," Frosst commanded.

I didn't know the man very well. I thought he was someone who knew what he was doing, but I didn't like the idea of flying under this thunderstorm. "Why don't we go around?" I asked.

"It's not necessary," he replied. "Ask for lower."

The Aztec is a tough airplane, but I knew from experience that thunderstorms contained killer turbulence, lightning, rain and hail. I decided that Frosst must know something about penetrating them that I didn't. There was one way to find out.

I requested and received a clearance to descend. We went down to minimum altitude for our sector and flew straight into the middle of the storm. We were slammed around badly. I kept waiting for Frosst to do something other than just ride it out and hope for the best. He didn't. By the time I realized that he had no secret tricks, we were half way through. There was no point in turning back.

The Aztec held together through the heavy rain and turbulence. When we popped out the other side, Frosst grinned and said, "I bet you'll never forget that one."

He was right. I didn't.

Charlie flew the same Aztec on a charter flight to Montreal in June 1968 with Hans Grob. Grob was an amiable Swiss who doubled at Peninsula as a charter pilot and an aircraft maintenance engineer specializing in aircraft electrics. His English was heavily accented, but he had an easy-going, professional manner about him. Charlie enjoyed flying with Hans.

On this trip we were carrying four businessmen. Two happened to be ex-Royal Canadian Air Force pilots. From Hamilton to Montreal, Hans flew the left seat while I worked the radios from the right. The flight was routine. We waited for the passengers there and headed back later that afternoon.

The weather was bad with low cloud and rain. It was my leg to fly from the left seat. We were still climbing out about 20 miles west of Montreal when the right engine started to hammer badly. The first thing I did was turn and look at Hans. "It's not going to run long like zat," he said. "Shuts it down. Ve go back."

I feathered the right propeller and shut down the engine. Hans called the radar controller, advised that we had one feathered and requested a turn around back to Montreal.

This was the real thing. We were flying in actual instrument conditions with one engine out and a full load of passengers. I had to concentrate hard to keep the airplane flying on the gauges but the Aztec has a better reserve of power than the Apache. Hans talked to me steadily but he never tried to take over. The pilots in the back did not say anything, but I felt that I had their undivided attention.

I could make the Aztec hold altitude, but I knew there would be only one approach for landing. We had to see the runway on the first shot. We couldn't risk having to do an overshoot and expect the airplane to climb.

The radar controller vectored us onto the localizer. We intercepted the glideslope in the cloud and started down. Hans called out the altitudes and I kept the needles centred. We broke out in time to see the runway. I throttled back, flared out and touched down. Everyone in the aircraft let out a collective sigh of relief.

We arranged for another airplane to come from Hamilton to pick them up. They said that would be fine as long as the other airplane had at least two engines and we would be the pilots. It was a nice endorsement of all the training and experience that went into completing that flight.

A subsequent teardown of the right engine revealed that one of the counterweights had separated from the crankshaft. Hans had been right. It would not have run for very long.

In March, 1969, Charlie flew as captain on a Peninsula Aztec on a trip with Terry Nunnemacher that was supposed to be from St. Catharines to Montreal and back. The trip illustrates a great deal about what it was like to fly charters in a medium-sized, piston-engine twin in the mid 1960s.

I got up early, drove over to Terry's house in St. Catharines, drove the 40 miles to Hamilton, preflighted the airplane and flew to St. Catharines to pick up the McFarlane brothers. I never had any trouble getting up early in the morning, but it makes it tough when the other end of the day gets long.

We flew the McFarlanes to Montreal for a meeting and waited for them until late afternoon. The weather forecast did not say that fog would blanket the west end of Lake Ontario, but it did. On the return trip, we shot two ADF approaches to Runway 06 at St. Catharines. We could see lights looking straight down over the city, but each time we descended into the fog, it was like flying into a milk bottle. We overshot the airport without seeing the runway and asked for a clearance to Toronto.

Despite the lower limits of Toronto's ILS approach, we still couldn't see anything at minimums. We could have tried again, but I knew at some point I would run out of energy and the airplane would run out of gas. I asked for a clearance to the nearest airport with better visibility. Kitchener, sitting on higher ground 40 miles west was open. We headed there and landed without any problem.

I arranged for a rental car for the passengers and booked into a hotel. I had been up 22 hours. The airplane was needed the next day, so on three hours sleep, I flew it back to Hamilton.

CHAPTER EIGHT

1968 - First Ferry

"It was one of those paint-yourself-into-a-corner flights."

Charlie Vaughn

₵harlie delivered new aircraft from the Piper factories to Hamilton for Glen White. He flew single-engine Cherokees from the plant in Vero Beach, Florida, and Aztecs from Lock Haven, Pennsylvania.

Trans Aircraft president Glen White paid $100 for each delivery. That was for everything: air fare, gas, hotel and food. By flying stand-by, I could go to Florida for $59. I would leave on an early morning flight out of Buffalo, New York, arriving in Vero Beach in time to do the twelve-hour flight without stopping overnight. The airplanes were full of fuel at the factory, so by timing the fuel burn to arrive in Hamilton empty, I could do the delivery at a break even cost providing I didn't eat too much or have to overnight for bad weather. It was no way to make money, but it was fun flying brand new airplanes.

I took my son Doug on one of the Florida trips. We picked up a single-engine Cherokee 235 and were airborne by noon. It turned into one of those "paint-yourself-into-a-corner" flights. We started out refreshed with full fuel, daylight and good weather. By the time we got to our last fuel stop in Williamsport, Pennsylvania, it was snowing and dark. We were both tired, but would I stop? I would now, but then I had this thing about not spending my own money on those flights.

We took off IFR for Hamilton with minimum fuel for Toronto as an alternate. The snowfall got heavier. When it looked like the visibility would be below Hamilton's half-mile minimum (it was after midnight and the weather office there was closed) I conceded that it would be acceptable to land at the United States Air Force base in Niagara Falls, New York, and have Robina drive across the border and pick us up. We had enough fuel to try one approach there and still go to Toronto if we missed.

It was one of those situations where you hope nothing goes wrong. You promise yourself that if you get out of this one, you'll leave yourself more options next time.

I shot the ILS approach to Niagara Falls. A bleary-eyed Doug was under orders to watch for the runway while I kept the needles centred. As we neared the missed approach point at 400 feet above the ground, the windshield brightened from the high intensity approach lights. I looked up and could just make out the runway. We landed all right and taxied in. We had to wait a few minutes before the customs officer arrived. I didn't mind. I think I would have sat in the cockpit for awhile anyway.

CHAPTER NINE

1969 - Float Flying

"That's the trouble with you big shot air transport pilots; you're colourblind."

Hugh McFarlane

The McFarlane brothers operated Canada Hair Cloth, a felt manufacturing company in St. Catharines. Hugh McFarlane was a licenced pilot and owned CF-PUS, a Cessna 185 on amphibious floats. He used it to commute to the family cottage on Lake of Bays in Central Ontario in good weather.

During the summer of 1969, Hugh McFarlane asked me to pick up Dr. George Callahan, a friend of his in Toronto in PUS and fly him to Cognawana Lodge in Quebec, north of Ottawa. Hugh had gone to the lodge a few days earlier with other friends.

I met George at the Toronto Island Airport in the late afternoon and headed northeast. The forecasts called for a large frontal system of bad weather around our destination. I couldn't get weather reports for that area, but I decided to go as far as we could VFR. The clouds were down to the top of the hills past Ottawa, so we had to fly up the Gatineau Valley to stay in the clear. It started to rain. I was pushing the weather and approaching darkness, but I could still see ahead and there was room in the valley to turn around so I continued.

I had never been to Cognawana Lodge, but Hugh had marked it on a map for me. He said that the lake was small, but he showed me that it was right beside Blue Lake, a popular fishing spot for lodge patrons. Hugh mentioned that there was a small strip of flat land between the lakes and there was usually a boat at either side.

The rain was steady on the windshield and it was getting dark when we arrived over the area. I map read my way as accurately as I could on an eight-mile-to-the-inch aeronautical chart, but I couldn't find the lodge. I did find Blue Lake. There was another seaplane docked there. I made the quick decision to land on Blue Lake and walk across to Cognawana.

I wasn't out of trouble yet. There was a thunderstorm approaching. It was windy and raining pretty hard. The only way I could dock with the other airplane there, was on my right side. I had to time my shutdown far enough back to climb out the left side, slide across under the engine on the float spreader bar and grab the dock, which I did. We tied up next to the other seaplane and unloaded our bags in the pouring rain.

George was still dressed in his Toronto suit and leather shoes, but he gamely followed me up a path that I told him would take us to Cognawana Lake. It seemed like a long uphill walk in the rain and mud compared to what Hugh had described. We were at the point when I was ready to give up and turn back when we came to a small lake. I could just make out the lights of what might be a lodge on the far shore, but we couldn't find a boat on our side.

We didn't have any choice but to go back. We knew there was a canoe with a motor sitting where we had tied up. George was good about it. He was soaked. He said it didn't matter if he waited or went. Either way, he was just going to get wetter. We headed back up the path.

It took us about an hour to get the canoe and motor and carry them back over the hilly portage to Cognawana. We launched the canoe and headed for the light. It turned out to be a private cottage, but the owner said we were on the right lake. He pointed to another set of lights across a bay and said it was the lodge.

A lady named Molly Robinson heard us coming and met us at the dock with a lantern. When we finally got inside, I told Hugh what I thought of his "short walk over flat ground" and gave him hell about the lack of a boat. He laughed it off in his good-natured way and poured us a stiff drink.

The next morning, Sid Turcotte, the owner of the other floatplane on the next lake, came into the lodge dining room for breakfast. When we were introduced by Hugh, I said that I had tied up next to him on Blue Lake.

"My aircraft isn't on Blue Lake," he replied. "It's over on Green Lake."

Hugh laughed. "That's the trouble with you big shot air transport pilots; you're colourblind."

One of Charlie's favourite stories about flying CF-PUS was a pleasure trip.

Robina had rented a cottage on Balsam Lake in a vacation area northeast of Toronto. The day before we were to go, the McFarlanes called to do a two-day flight to Winnipeg in a Piper Aztec that they had leased. I explained that I had family commitments up north.

"No problem," says Hugh. "We'll have you back in good time from the trip and you can fly PUS from Muskoka to join your family at the cottage."

I agreed.

Robina headed north with the boys in the car and I flew the Aztec from St. Catharines to Winnipeg, stopping for passengers and fuel at Toronto, Muskoka and Thunder Bay. I stayed overnight in Winnipeg and flew back with the same stops the next day. The flying was hard work. I had to navigate through a cold front complete with thunderstorms both ways without benefit of weather radar. It was late afternoon when we got back to Muskoka. Hugh flew the Aztec on to St. Catharines leaving me to fly his Cessna 185 east to Balsam Lake.

There was plenty of daylight left, but the cold front was expected to be approaching the area the same time I was. The forecast was accurate. When I arrived at Balsam Lake, I could see a monster thunderstorm approaching from the northwest. I had asked Robina how I would know which cottage they would be in. She had said, "It's the one with the green roof on the south shore. It sticks out. When you fly over, we'll wave to you from the dock."

I should have known better. I'd flown to vacation lakes many times. From the air, the cottages are lined up along the shoreline by the hundreds all tucked under the trees. Most of them have a green roof. At Balsam Lake, no cottage stood out as the right one and there was no one standing on a dock. The storm was getting bigger, blacker and closer. At the far end of the lake, there was a small boy fishing off a dock. I didn't have much time to waste so I landed near him and shut down within shouting distance. I asked him if he knew where the cottage in question was. "Sure mister," he replied. "I'll show you if you take me for a ride."

He seemed to be oblivious to the storm which was now just a few miles away. I didn't have time for rides and I told him so.

"No ride, no directions," he replied.

The little twit was only about twelve-years-old, but I admired his spunk. I took him for a quick hop around the lake. By now Robina and the boys were waving from the dock. I landed immediately. By the time I tied up, the storm hit with pouring rain and gusty winds.

When I got into the cottage, Robina said, "I told you that you wouldn't have any trouble finding it."

I had to drive the kid back to his place.

CHAPTER TEN

1971 - Air Racing

"I'd do it again in a minute."
John Clement

On July 1 and 2, 1971, fifty-eight aircraft departed from RAF Station Abingdon, Berkshire, outside of London, England, on an air race to Victoria, British Columbia. Race aircraft Number 74 was piloted by a farmer from Niagara named Charlie Vaughn. His co-pilot was John Clement, a lawyer from Niagara Falls.

Entering the race was John's idea. He had heard about it and suggested we enter. My reply was that I had never flown across water bigger than the Great Lakes; I had never been off the North American continent; and I had never been in an air race, but I was interested.

"Good enough," John said, "I'll send away for an application."

The Great London to Victoria Air Race was conceived by Information Canada Expositions as a method of involving the rest of Canada in British Columbia's Centennial celebrations. The idea won the sponsorship of the Canadian and B.C. governments. The Race was organized by the Royal Canadian Flying Clubs Association under the direction of Bill Paris with the assistance of the Royal Aero Club in England and a cast of hundreds along the route.

The race was open to civilian airplanes grouped into four classes:

"A" - single-engine piston up to 5,000 pounds;
"B" - twin-engine piston up to 12,500 pounds;
"C" - turbo-prop or supercharged up to 12,500 pounds;

"D" - pure jet up to 30,000 pounds.

The 5,787-mile distance from Abingdon to Victoria was divided into six stages, the longest by far being the 3,342-mile first leg from Abingdon to Quebec City.

The prize money totalled $170,000. It included a $50,000 prize for first overall, stage winner prizes and class winner prizes. The race attracted 79 entries from nine countries.

In 1971, John Clement was a lawyer living and laughing in Niagara Falls, Ontario. He was round and quick-witted. He was serious only when absolutely necessary. His measure of any activity was its potential for having fun. As a pleasure pilot, Clement had neither the qualifications nor the aspirations to compete in a transatlantic air race on his own, but the idea of doing it appealed to him.

Clement met Charlie in 1959. He was learning how to fly at the St. Catharines Flying Club and Charlie was instructing on Sundays.

"According to my log book," Clement recalls, "our first lesson together was April 12, 1959. It was in an Aeronca Champ, exercises 12 and 13. What's that; stalls and spins? Sure, leave it to Charlie to teach stalls and spins on a Sunday. Nobody told him that Sunday comes after Saturday night."

Clement went on to receive his pilot licence and continued as an active pilot and member of the Flying Club. By 1970, he and Charlie were both members of the Club's board of directors. The two men developed a good friendship.

Charlie's biggest concern about the race was how they were going to pay for it. Clement had already convinced himself they would win some of the prize money. To satisfy Charlie, he worked out what proved to be an accurate budget of $10,000. It was an amount that neither man was capable of covering on his own.

At the time, Charlie was still flying frequent charters for Glen White's Peninsula Air Service in Hamilton. One of his regular passengers was Doug Hatch, president of Brights Wines in Niagara Falls. It was Clement's idea that they approach Hatch with the suggestion that Brights sponsor their entry in the race. Both men knew Hatch personally but they proposed the sponsorship not as a favour, but as an advertising and business promotion. They told Hatch that they would attend receptions arranged for Brights' customers when the race made its several stops across Canada.

Hatch bought the pitch to the tune of $5,000. Clement then met with John Shepherd, a tax lawyer, who agreed that their personal investments would represent a legitimate business expense for income tax purposes. This was on the reasonable expectation of earning prize money. The two pilots decided they could live with the idea of paying $2,500 each out of their own pockets in the unlikely event that they didn't win any prize money.

They applied for Race Number 74, which coincided with two of Brights brands, 74 Sherry and 74 Port. This allowed the company to promote "the Flight of Brights 74" without infringing on advertising bans on alcohol.

Charlie approached Glen White about leasing an airplane. The long-time Canadian Piper Aircraft Distributor immediately offered a brand new Piper Aztec E. The popular six-place airplane had a maximum gross weight of 5,200 pounds and was powered by two, normally-aspirated, 250-hp Lycoming engines. Piper advertised that it would cruise up to 203 mph.

Always the businessman, White said they could lease the airplane as long as they paid the cost of transoceanic insurance, which his coverage didn't include.

The insurance company was willing to add the ocean crossing to the policy for the first-timers for an extra $2,500, one quarter of their entire race budget. The two pilots had no choice but to be happy to get the coverage at any price.

The next hurdle was navigation. The VOR transmitters that were the mainstay of continental navigation in North America were only good for short range, "line-of-sight" reception. Marine Loran navigation had not yet been adopted for aviation and Global Positioning satellites did not exist.

I spoke to Tom Thususka. Tom was the airline pilot from St. Catharines who was hired by Trans Canada Airlines at the time I was rejected. I asked him where we might find a transatlantic navigator to teach us. He posted a notice on the company bulletin board. It was answered by Ray English, a TCA navigator. Ray was willing to teach ocean navigation in exchange for multi-engine training. He was looking to move into a pilot's position with the airline, which he eventually did.

Ray was great. He supplied us with all the know-how, charts and information that we would need. He said that navigating across the Atlantic was a combination of Consol long-range ADF and dead reckoning. The powerful Non-Directional Beacon transmitters on the coasts of Canada, Greenland, Iceland and the U.K. provided coverage much of the way. "The rest of the time," Ray said, "Over a long distance, the wind tends to average out so you just hold the heading and keep the faith."

In the spirit of the low budget operation, Charlie drew from his long list of aviation friends to help with the preparations for the race. Carm Daw, a local Niagara furnace contractor, fabricated a pair of 75-gallon cabin fuel tanks in his sheet metal shop. Keith Mitchell, a St. Catharines aircraft mechanic who worked for Genaire, a local aviation maintenance specialty shop, installed the tanks according to drawings obtained from Piper. Together with the regular 140 U.S. gallons of fuel carried in the wings, it was planned that the cabin tanks would give the Aztec a twelve-hour range at full power. Charlie had spoken to Lycoming engineers in Williamsport, Pennsylvania. They had said that full throttle in level flight would not hurt those engines.

With full fuel in all the tanks, the airplane's takeoff weight went 500 pounds over the maximum allowable, so they test flew the installation with partial fuel. John remarked that the caps on the cabin tanks were hard to get off after each flight. Neither man thought much about it since the installation seemed to work fine.

Bob Simmons, a Woodstock-based businessman/pilot who flew his Piper Navajo everywhere, loaned the two air racers his ocean crossing life raft and survival gear.

A Toronto-based avionics mechanic gave Charlie and Clement a good price on a used High Frequency radio. HF communications equipment was a requirement for transoceanic flight. The old radio was a fixed crystal set, but Ray English had given them a list of the frequency crystals they would need to buy. The crystals were expensive but necessary.

Charlie arranged for the radio to be installed in the Aztec in Hamilton. In the process, the avionics mechanic broke one of the circuit breakers on the electrical panel. Unknown to the pilots, he replaced it with the only breaker that he had; one that was a smaller size.

On June 22, Brights held a "send off" reception for the "Flight of Brights 74."

They departed from St. Catharines the next day. The race was scheduled to start on July 1. Charlie and Clement planned to take two or three days to get to London, leaving them plenty of time to either work on problems along the way or to enjoy London for a few days.

They didn't fill all the fuel tanks because they didn't want to push their luck departing overloaded from St. Catharines on a hot day. The first destination was Goose Bay, Labrador, their jump-off point for crossing the Atlantic. They quickly settled into a routine. Charlie flew from the left seat while Clement navigated and managed the fuel from the right.

Although Charlie had never been across the ocean, long flights were not new to him. He had flown thousands of hours all over North America. He was happy. They were finally under way after months of planning. The weather was good and everything in the new airplane was working well. He settled into monitoring the instruments while the autopilot carried them east at 9,000 feet.

Once they were established in cruise flight, Clement switched from the airplane's wings to the cabin ferry tanks. The ferry fuel fed directly into the right engine's gascolator, a water separator in the right wing. To draw from it, John opened a valve on the line from the cabin tanks, switched the fuel selector for the right engine to "off" and turned the left engine fuel selector to "crossfeed". The only problem with this arrangement was that there were no fuel level sensors in the ferry tanks. With the wing tanks switched off, the fuel gauges in the instrument panel in front of Clement read "empty". To monitor the fuel level in the cabin tanks, they had to be dipped. There was a small space between the top of the tanks and the roof of the cabin. It was Clement's job to unfold a carpenter's rule into the opening in each ferry tank every half hour and log the fuel consumption. This, plus the fact that he was navigating in good weather, did not keep the good-timer occupied for very long. His other problem was that he couldn't smoke. Since he was sitting in front of 150 gallons of high octane aviation fuel, he had to give up cigarettes for the trip.

John soon decided that this air racing was boring. Staring at fuel gauges reading 'empty' really bothered him, especially since he had little else to do except dream about having a smoke and dip the tanks.

I was happy to fly for hours without saying much, but John told joke after raunchy joke. At one point I told him that I wasn't interested in getting into trouble with women if we got a few days in London. He asked why I thought I needed to mention that. I didn't answer him right away so he asked what I did want to get into trouble with in London.

"Nothing," I replied. "What was the fuel level on that last dip?"

"I'm not telling you," he said. "You'll know soon enough when they're empty."

And so it went all the way to Goose Bay, and beyond. The banter was classical John Clement and Charlie was the perfect straight man.

The flight to Goose Bay took 5:45 for an average ground speed of 190 knots and a fuel consumption of 14.7 U.S. gallons per hour per engine. The weather was good, so they decided to continue to Iceland after refuelling at Goose Bay. They had all the tanks filled. The airplane weighed 500 pounds over its normal maximum gross when the pilots departed for the first leg across the North Atlantic. The air was cool for June and they took off using less than half of Goose Bay's 6,000-foot runway.

On the climbout to 9,000 feet, they crossed the rugged Labrador coastline and headed out over the cold North Atlantic. When they were established at cruising altitude, Clement switched to the cabin tanks and then unwound the HF trailing antennae. He tried to call the Gander Oceanic Controller on the HF. The radio didn't work.

We could hear people talking on it; Alaska, Kuala Lumpur, South Africa, but we never heard a reply when we called the Atlantic Ocean controllers.

The transatlantic regulations required aircraft to be HF equipped. It was, but it didn't work. They continued using the VHF radios and relayed position reports via airliners flying overhead when they were out of range of the ground stations.

About an hour off the coast of Labrador, both engines quit. They stopped suddenly and within seconds of each other. Charlie set the Aztec up for a glide toward the North Atlantic and yelled at Clement, "Pull the stoppers on the ferry tanks!"

The first thing that had jumped into his mind was not the time-honoured checklist memorized by all multi-engine pilots, but Clement's comment about the negative pressure in the cabin fuel tanks.

I didn't want to switch to the wing tanks without confirming the problem. The propellers were windmilling and we had plenty of altitude. While I flew a gliding turn back toward the coast, John pulled the plug on the first tank. There was a "whoosh" and a "bang". The tanks had not been venting properly. When they were partially filled, there was enough air in them to allow the fuel to draw, but when they were full, it didn't take long for the fuel flow to stop. The "whoosh, bang" noise was the air rushing in and the sides of the tanks popping back out. Both windmilling engines immediately restarted on their own.

They climbed back to altitude and resumed course for Iceland. Although it was late in the day, the summer sun hung in the northwest sky as the flight of Brights 74 crossed the southern tip of Greenland and flew up its icy east coast.

The mountains of Greenland loomed forbidding but spectacular on our left. On the map, it looked like we should be leaving the Greenland coast as we flew northeast to Iceland, but in the air it appeared that our distance from the mountains never diminished. I turned the airplane 10 degrees to the right. I didn't appreciate the illusion of closeness created by the size of Greenland's 10,000-foot high mountains. The turn didn't seem to make much difference but I resisted turning any further. Eventually we slowly drew away from the mountains.

The two pilots did not realize it at the time, but the sweat produced by the fuel flow incident was the last time they would be warm during the Atlantic crossing. Although it was June, it was minus four degrees Celsius at 9,000 feet. The sun was sinking low off their left side when the circuit breaker for the gasoline heater popped.

We gave the breaker time to cool and then reset it. It popped again. The last thing I wanted was a fire over the North Atlantic. We left it alone after that. The temperature in the cabin dropped rapidly. There was a fresh air inlet open behind the ferry tanks to vent the fuel smell and we couldn't reach to close it. All of our extra clothes were stored in the nose baggage compartment to help offset the weight of the ferry fuel. The only thing we had to put on over our summer clothes were plastic garbage bags. We wrapped aeronautic charts around our legs and feet.

At first, the two pilots made fun of their problem. The peanut butter and jam sandwiches they had saved for supper were frozen solid.

"These don't taste as good when you have to suck on them first," Clement joked. "The first thing I'm going to do when we get to Iceland is hire the two biggest hookers I can find and sleep between them to get warm."

As the sun touched the horizon to the north, they still had a couple of hours to go. The temperature in the cockpit continued to drop.

Clement looked at the ocean and mused, "I don't know about you, Charlie, but I wouldn't mind another double engine failure about now. I think that water would be warmer than we are."

Charlie smiled but he knew they were in trouble. He was finding it difficult to concentrate enough to copy air traffic control clearances as they were relayed from airliners flying overhead.

During the last hour, I lost the feeling in my feet. I was so cold that I couldn't talk properly. We didn't want to descend for warmer air, because we needed to pick up the VOR signal from Reykjavik as soon as possible. When we did finally receive it, we saw that my 10 degree heading correction had taken us 30 miles to the right of our intended course. Thankfully the weather was good enough for a visual approach. I couldn't feel the rudder pedals under my feet so I asked John to follow me on the controls.

As soon as they touched down, Clement popped the door open on the Aztec to let in the warmer air. They taxied to the ramp.

All we could think of was a warm bath.

They were met by Sven Bjornson, the manager of the Flight Services fixed base operation at Reykjavik. Bjornson could see that the two pilots were frozen and arranged a ride for them over to the Loftleider Hotel right away.

They still weren't home free. Clement and Charlie arrived at the hotel still dressed in garbage bags. They looked like scarecrows and walked like robots operating on weak batteries. When they shivered to a stop in front of the reception desk. The female night clerk looked at them nervously and said, "I'm sorry, we don't have any rooms."

John didn't hesitate for a minute. He asked to speak to the manager. The girl went and got him. We explained our situation; and he gave us a room. I'm telling you, if you've never seen two guys trying to get into a one-man shower together, you should have been there.

They stayed a day and a half to recover and distribute some champagne. The only permanent damage was frost bite to two toes on Charlie's left foot. The champagne was Brights. They carried a case of it to give to the airport staff on their way over to England on the theory that it might speed up their refuelling stops during the air race.

While they were in Iceland, Charlie checked the ferry tank installation for the cause of the negative pressure. He saw that the rubber vent tubes for the two cabin tanks went through the floor of the Aztec and trailed six inches below. Genaire had installed them according to Piper's drawings. Charlie cut the tubes off one inch below the floor at a 45 degree angle to the oncoming airflow. They never had another problem with the fuel after that.

There was no one at Reykjavik who could repair the circuit breaker for the heater. On June 25, the two pilots departed for Prestwick, Scotland, looking like Pillsbury dough boys in their multiple layers of clothing.

For navigation on that leg, we used long range ADF signals and Consol charts. By counting the dots on the beat frequency oscillation, it was possible to determine a bearing from the station. Bearings from two or more stations gave a position cross fix. It was a monotonous way to navigate, but it worked. More important, it gave John something to do.

We relayed position reports every five degrees of longitude via the airliners flying overhead. The airline pilots were friendly and helpful. One of the Pan Am pilots asked what we were doing, so we explained the race. We told him we were spreading champagne on the way over and racing back. He said, "Come on up, we've got the girls if you have the champagne."

It took them just over five hours to fly to Prestwick. They cleared customs and departed for London's Gatwick Airport and two days of sightseeing.

On June 27, they flew the Aztec to Oxford Kiddlington Airport north of London where they had arranged for a Piper Service Centre to check the airplane over, change the oil and fix the heater. On June 29, they transferred the airplane to Abingdon Airport near London, the start line for the race.

At Abingdon, they met the other race entrants. The main topic of conversation was the handicapping system. It was based on the manufacturer's published maximum cruise speed for the aircraft. Since Piper was among the more optimistic manufacturers, Charlie and Clement realized before they started that they could not possibly win the race.

The best airspeed that we could get on the way over was around 150 knots using full throttle at 9,000 feet. The Pilot Operating Handbook said it was 175 knots. It was obvious, that to win the race, an entrant needed a turbocharged or turbine airplane that could be over boosted to beat the manufacturer's specs.

Race day was July 2. Brights 74 took off in clear weather mid-morning. Charlie and Clement flew non-stop to Reykjavik in seven hours without incident. They spent some of that time rehearsing each of their jobs on the ground at Reykjavik. They couldn't do anything about their poor handicap in the air, but they were allowed one hour for each stop. If they could beat that, they would make up time.

Charlie flew a high speed descent and a straight-in approach to the runway. He let the speed carry after landing and did a quick turn off to the ramp. He shut down and both men jumped out of the airplane. Charlie ran into the terminal building to clear customs while Clement stayed with the airplane and supervised the refuelling. The planning and the gifts of champagne on the way over worked. They were airborne for Goose Bay, Labrador, in 30 minutes.

The weather stayed good until Greenland, then we couldn't avoid flying in cloud. We started picking up some soft ice. I made the mistake of operating the leading edge boots too soon. They inflated and pushed the ice out without breaking it off. The ice continued to build until our airspeed dropped to 100 knots. This was our longest leg of the race. I knew we would run out of fuel flying at a reduced speed and full power. We had to descend to find warm air to melt the ice, but that meant going below the minimum altitude near Greenland. We determined our position to be still over the ocean so I descended, but I didn't like doing it. I had a vivid memory of the mountains along the Greenland coast.

As soon as the ice was mostly gone, we climbed back up again. The airplane immediately picked up more ice. I was able to shed it from the leading edges but it continued to build on the non-booted parts of the airplane. Our speed slowly dropped. I tried to raise the U.S. military base at Sondre Strom on the emergency VFR frequency 121.5 MHz several times to check the weather ahead without success. I left the radio turned up. A voice boomed through the speaker loud and clear, "Charlie, is that you?"

It sounded so close, I turned to John and said, "It must be God."

"Must be," John replied, "no one else seems to know we're here."

It wasn't God; it was Ron Stewart. Ron was an Air Canada pilot from St. Catharines. He was flying a McDonnell Douglas DC-8 overhead on the way to Toronto. He had recognized my voice. I called him back and he asked if there was anything he could do for us. I said it would help if he could get weather for Goose Bay and the surrounding area, which he did. It sounded like we had been through the worst of it, so we decided to continue. I was telling Ron about the air race when an emergency locator transmitter signal from another aircraft came on the frequency. I quickly asked him to call my dad when he got home and relay that we were all right and then I signed off.

The flight of Brights 74 was down to 100 knots indicated airspeed, but they were doing better than some of the single-engine race entrants. The emergency locator transmitter signal was from Race Aircraft Number 2, a Bellanca Viking that had run out of fuel while the two pilots were trying to find Narsarssuaq, Greenland, in the bad weather. The airplane had been ditched successfully in the ocean and the pilots were subsequently rescued.

A funny sidelight to Charlie's conversation with Ron Stewart, was the airline pilot's phone call to Charlie's dad. He told Charlie about it after the race.

The phone call request had been a spur-of-the-moment thing. Charlie thought it would be nice if the senior Vaughn received a message from his air racing son from over the Atlantic. But Bill Vaughn Sr. had trouble understanding the situation. He knew Stewart's father, who was also a farmer, and he knew Charlie was not home, but that's about all he understood. Stewart called him, identified himself and said that Charlie was flying over Greenland and was okay.

"Who's this?"

"Ron Stewart. George Stewart's boy, Ron."

"Hello George, what can I do for you?"

"It's Ron, Mr. Vaughn. I'm calling to tell you that I talked to your son, Charlie. He was approaching Greenland and was okay."

"What's Charlie doing?"

"He's flying in the air race, sir, but he's okay."

"Okay, okay, George. Thanks for calling. You tell Charlie to come home. We got work to do."

Brights 74 was slowed by a good load of ice, but it wasn't getting any worse. Charlie knew they were going to make it.

Clement had other things on his mind. He hadn't been to the bathroom since Abingdon, England. He was about to wet himself. Charlie had warned him not to drink much on the long legs and he hadn't, but it had been fifteen hours since his last pee in England. He was in pain, but he wasn't going to let on to Charlie. Clement decided if Charlie had the endurance of a two-humped camel, then he wasn't going to give him the satisfaction of knowing he had a big problem. Besides, he knew that Charlie couldn't do anything to help him.

The weather was bad enough that Charlie flew a radar-vectored approach into Goose Bay. He kept the power on trying to make up for lost time. They landed with an 8:35 flight time from Reykjavik. It had been over 16 hours since Clement had been to the bathroom.

As soon as we were rolling to a stop on the ramp, John opened the door, jumped out, unzipped his fly and started to drill a big hole in the asphalt under the tail of the airplane. I hopped out behind him and yelled, "What are you doing?"

"If you have to ask, you're too young to fly with me," John replied and kept on drilling.

"You can't do that here; they've got washrooms inside,' I said.

"Maybe you can hold it for 16 hours, but I can't," he said.

"I used the washroom in the terminal building at Reykjavik," I told him.

"We're in an air race and you pissed in Iceland? Now you tell me! Go clear customs."

I think he was still going when I came back out.

The two pilots still hadn't finished the first leg of the race which ended in Quebec City. They refuelled with enough to finish the day, but planned "dummy" stops along the St. Lawrence River at Sept Iles, Baie Comeau and Mont Joli. All they needed at each stop was to have their race card stamped. This would give them an hour's credit at each one. Charlie said that by the time they got to Mont Joli, the race officials were into the "dummy" stop idea and were waiting to stamp the cards on the edge of the runway. They completed the four hops in 2:55.

The finish line was the Cartier Bridge at Quebec City. They dove over it, pulled up and landed at the airport.

The race organizers had arranged for the entrants to stay over for a day and a half at the Chateau Frontenac in downtown Quebec City. The rest gave them a chance to find out what happened to the ones who hadn't made it.

The stop was also a chance for Brights to invite their local distributors to a reception to meet the pilots of Brights 74. The winery's public relations man, Wilf Morgan, travelling ahead on the airlines, arranged a party at each stop across Canada.

The leg the next day was the shortest of the race. Charlie and Clement flew Quebec City to Ottawa in 1:25. Ceremonies had been arranged at the nation's capital for that evening in recognition of the federal government's support of the race.

One of the other Piper Aztecs in the race was flown by Powder Puff Derby Race veterans Margaret Mead and Fran Bera. They were a fun pair, so John and I invited them to the Brights reception in Ottawa. One of the Brights people took a liking to Fran and she did nothing to discourage him. Apparently they partied until the early hours of the morning. When Fran staggered into bed, Margaret knocked on our door, and tongue-in-cheek, accused us of sabotaging her crew.

The next day's leg was to Winnipeg, Manitoba. They loaded up with fuel so they could do quick "dummy" stops at Sault Ste. Marie and Thunder Bay, Ontario. The weather was good but the headwinds were strong. The Brights 74 team kept the airplane at low level to stay out of as much wind as possible. By the afternoon, Charlie and Clement were flying right down the middle of Lake Superior 50 feet above the waves. It was warm, windy and turbulent. About half way along, they hit an extra sharp bump in the air. One engine quit. The airplane was still heavy with fuel. It would not hold altitude on one engine. Charlie looked down at the throttles. One was at idle. The last updraft/downdraft combination had forced the throttle back. Charlie moved the lever up and the engine came back to life. He tightened the lever friction and it didn't happen again.

On July 6, the race continued from Winnipeg to Calgary, Alberta, with a "dummy" stop in Regina, Saskatchewan. Charlie and Clement again flew the Aztec at full throttle on the deck to maximize their groundspeed into the wind. The ride was hot and bumpy. Flying at low level put them out of range of any radio navigation aids. It made map reading more difficult, but it was all they could do to make up time.

It didn't help. The more they raced, the further they trailed the leaders. They were racing against their own optimistic aircraft specifications and they couldn't beat them. But they didn't quit. Although they were out of the prize money, they raced against the pilots in the other poorly-handicapped airplanes and for the pride of being in the race and finishing.

The last leg was from Calgary to Victoria, British Columbia. They went for altitude to clear the Rocky Mountains and were treated to a front-row view of the world's most beautiful mountains. They crossed the finish line at Trial Island and landed at Victoria International Airport.

Their total flight time from London to Victoria was 32:45. The official standing of the Brights 74 entry was 13th out of 25 in Class B.

Charlie and Clement were met in Victoria by Charlie's wife Robina and his son Dennis. They stayed for the three days of activities that were part of the B.C. Centennial celebrations. These included the wind-up Air Race banquet.

The two pilots had arranged for the Aztec's seats to be shipped to Victoria. They had the cabin fuel tanks removed and the seats installed in their place. The day after the banquet, the five of them headed back to Niagara.

"I'd do it again in a minute," John declared at the end of the race. I agreed with him. I relive that air race every time I cross the Atlantic."

CHAPTER ELEVEN

1971 - Black September

"It was not a pretty sight. By the time I arrived, the bodies had been removed, but there were bits of clothing and upholstery everywhere."

Charlie Vaughn

During much of the 1960s, Charlie was a member of the board of directors of the St. Catharines Flying Club. This was largely a thankless, unpaid job reserved for local enthusiasts with a desire to contribute to the aviation community. In 1971, Charlie was named president of the board of directors.

The early '70s were good times for general aviation. The Canadian economy was rolling, the cost of fuel was still cheap and learning to fly for pleasure was a tax deductible educational expense. The St. Catharines Flying Club's school was busy with new students learning to fly and a growing list of members renting aircraft. The club had a full-time manager, four full-time flying instructors, two part-time instructors and several support staff. There was enough business for the club to have purchased four brand new Piper Cherokees the year before. It owned a Cessna 172, leased a Piper Apache for multi-engine training and a Champion Citabria for aerobatic training. The club was the only aircraft operator on the airport. The flying lessons and aircraft rental were its main businesses, but it also had a licence to provide charter flights using the flying school fleet. Fuel sales, aircraft storage and maintenance rounded out the activity.

On the second Sunday in September, the club hosted what had become Canada's third largest annual air show. The 1971 version attracted top name acts, including Art Scholl, Gene Soucy and the Royal Air Force Red Arrows.

As club president, it was Charlie's job to lead the board of directors which set the club's policies, ratified capital expenditures and approved the work of the manager who handled the day-to-day affairs. The club was busy, but seemed to run well under Manager Peter McNaughton. Charlie went on the London to Victoria Air Race without worrying too much about the club activities.

Three events, or more accurately, two events and one non-event in September would show Charlie that there could be a whole lot of worry for the president of a large, busy flying club.

During the second week of September, volunteer club members prepared for the air show. The staff continued with the flying operation. On the Friday before the show, a Toronto businessman called for a charter flight for Saturday. He and a buddy wanted to go to a horse race in Fort Erie and one in lower New York state on the same day. They asked if the club would fly them from one race to another and then back that night. The enthusiastic answer from Larry Holloway, one of the young flying instructors anxious to build flying time in the twin-engined Apache, was "Yes". Holloway was scheduled to appear in the air show flying a formation demonstration of the school aircraft with four other instructors on the Sunday. He said he would be back in time.

He never made it.

On the Saturday morning, Holloway flew to Fort Erie and picked up the two passengers. He took a young airport enthusiast with him, the brother of the club's lineman.

A large warm front was moving up from the south. Holloway did not have an instrument rating and the club's charter operating certificate was for visual flight rules only, but he decided to give it a try. He got as far as the hills of Pennsylvania before low cloud forced him to fly down a narrow valley. He entered cloud to make room to turn around, but didn't make enough. The airplane slammed into a forested ridge. Everyone on board was killed.

No one saw the Apache go in. Holloway had been flying too low to be seen on radar. He had not declared an emergency. He was on a flight plan and had been talking to a flight service station about the weather earlier. When the airplane became overdue, the American authorities decided it was down in the hills, but could not pinpoint exactly where. The bad weather and approaching darkness precluded any kind of search that day.

Back in St. Catharines, the final preparations were being made for the air show. Word got back that the Apache was missing. There was nothing anyone could do but worry.

The warm front moved into St. Catharines Saturday night and stayed all day Sunday. The bad weather turned the air show into a non-event. The rain let up in the morning, but the cloud stayed at 500 feet. Only two aircraft flew the air show schedule for the benefit of the few hundred people who came to watch. The Canadian Armed Forces rescue helicopter did a hover demonstration and the incredible Art Scholl flew his entire routine, disappearing into the cloud during the top half of his loops, rolls and hammerheads.

The club lost a lot of morale and money on that show. The huge amount of volunteer work went down the drain. Sponsors for the main acts covered that cost, but the hundreds of other things had to be paid out of the club's coffers. Repeated calls to the American authorities responsible for searching for the Apache produced no new news.

The next day, the weather improved. Charlie authorized the manager to add the club's assets to the search for the Apache. It meant cancelling all the revenue flights and paying the cost of flying the club aircraft around the search area, but it was a positive action to help find the missing instructor and his passengers.

Holloway was a popular member of the club's staff. The instructors volunteered to fly the aircraft and a long list of club members volunteered to ride along as spotters. Six club airplanes and several privately owned aircraft from St. Catharines flew down to Pennsylvania for five days in a row, joining the search conducted by the American Civil Air Patrol. They didn't find anything.

By the end of the week, Charlie and McNaughton decided to put the airplanes back on the line for flying lessons. The

Civil Air Patrol called off its search without spotting any sign of a crash.

A week after the search was terminated, Charlie allowed the manager to attend the Annual Meeting of the Royal Canadian Flying Club Association where he was to be awarded the Yorath Trophy for managing the most efficiently run flying club. Charlie went back to work on the farm harvesting grapes.

While the manager was away at the convention, a sixteen-year-old boy who had never taken a flying lesson in his life was successful in renting one of the club's new Piper Cherokees and getting it airborne. It was a well planned stunt. The youngster had been flying with Henry Weiler. Weiler was a long-time fixture at the club. He spent his sunny Sundays canvassing cars in the airport parking lot for people who would go with him for a sightseeing flight. Weiler would rent an aircraft from the club and take them for a ride over Niagara Falls.

The kid had flown with Weiler twice. Each time he watched the old pilot carefully. Henry happily explained everything that he did. Next the youngster borrowed a couple of pilot log books from the shelves in the club lounge. He bought a new log book for himself. He knew from watching Weiler rent airplanes that the staff were trained to check the member's recent log book entries to make sure they had flown in the last couple of months. The club was busy, but it was still small enough that the staff knew the rental customers. Nobody checked for a membership card or pilot licence because no one had ever tried to rent a club airplane without them.

The would-be pilot called the club on a Saturday when he knew the regular receptionist was off and booked an aircraft in his own name for the next Saturday at noon. That was the day of the Annual Grape and Wine Fall Festival parade.

He presented himself at the club's flight desk with a passenger. Leon Evans, the chief flying instructor, was off for lunch, leaving George Bobro, the most junior instructor, on duty for signing out aircraft rentals. The kid showed Bobro his log book. In it he had faked a long list of current entries, including checkout flights with aircraft and instructors familiar to Bobro. George didn't recognize the kid, but being relatively new himself, he had no reason to doubt the log book. He signed him out.

The youngster did everything that Weiler had shown him, including a pre-flight inspection. He even explained what he was doing to his passenger who was a younger kid that he had met in downtown St. Catharines earlier that morning. He had asked his new friend if he wanted to go for an airplane ride. The youngster said, "Yes."

The first indication that something was wrong came from the air traffic controller in the tower. He phoned the club on a direct line and asked why one of the Cherokees had taken off going the wrong way on the active runway without any radio contact.

Before Bobro had much time to absorb that call, the police phoned from downtown St. Catharines to ask why one of the club's airplanes was flying erratically about 200 feet above the Grape and Wine Festival Parade.

CFI Leon Evans arrived from lunch just ahead of the RCMP. He was able to figure out what was going on by questioning Bobro. The tower controller continued to radio the airplane with no response. He instructed other aircraft to stay clear of the area. There was nothing anyone could do except wait for the kid to come down. They didn't have to wait long.

The youngster aimed for the airport, into wind this time, with cruise power still set on the throttle. He hit the runway nosewheel first at over 120 mph. The Cherokee did a series of porpoises until the nosewheel folded back, the prop hit and the engine stopped. The airplane skidded off the side of the runway into the infield. Evans followed the sliding wreck in the airport's crash jeep. Both kids jumped out of the wrecked airplane. They would have been unhurt except a furious Leon Evans decked the pilot with a punch to the face.

Charlie arrived to find the RCMP interviewing the two young birdmen in the manager's office with Evans. The situation was not good. The club had a wrecked airplane flown by an unlicensed high school student authorized by a staff member. The kid had a growing black eye administered by another staff member. The potential for some expensive, possibly uninsured, litigation against the club was great.

Then the young pilot's parents arrived. When they were informed of what had happened, they immediately offered to pay all damages if the Club would not press charges. They didn't want their son to have a criminal record.

I took them up on it right away. I even pushed it a little further by telling them the expenses would include the cost of the airplane and the lost rental time while it was being repaired or replaced. They agreed. The RCMP officer asked me to let him know when the debt had been settled.

The following week the wreck of the Flying Club's Apache was found in Pennsylvania by a deer hunter walking through the hills. It was not far off its known course, but the airplane had ploughed into a near vertical ridge and then slid down among the trees. It had not been a survivable accident. Charlie flew down to the scene of the crash.

It was not a pretty sight. By the time I arrived, the bodies had been removed, but there were bits of clothing and upholstery everywhere. I talked to the hunter who found the wreck. He was quite graphic about the scene when he first saw it.

The club was closed for the day of the funeral. A memorial fund was started in the name of the two club members who died in the crash. The money was used to buy emergency locator transmitters for each of the club aircraft.

A few weeks later, the Cherokee damaged during the Grape and Wine Parade incident was back on the line at the Club. The one-time aviator's parents paid the hefty bill promptly. When the RCMP were notified of this, they arrested the youngster and charged him with operating an aircraft without a pilot's licence. He pleaded guilty and received a suspended sentence.

The financial strain on the club during September caused Charlie to become more involved in the daily affairs than he would have liked, but it revealed that despite a busy year, the club had not been in very good financial shape. Peter McNaughton was asked to resign as club manager.

CHAPTER TWELVE

1973 - Seaplane Racing

"Hello Charlie? It's John. We're going racing again."
John Clement

In 1973, Floyd Carson proposed The Great Burlington Centennial Seaplane Race as part of the City of Burlington's Centennial celebrations. Burlington sits on the west end of Lake Ontario across from Hamilton. Carson was a Burlington-based aircraft broker who had competed in the London to Victoria Air Race. In honour of the year, he outlined a three-day, 1,973 nm triangular course with overnight stops in Kenora, Ontario, and Ottawa, and a return to Burlington.

John Clement and Charlie had agreed at the end of the London to Victoria Race that if they had the opportunity to do it again, they would. The next time they would be a lot wiser about picking an airplane, working the rules to their advantage and winning. Burlington was their chance.

The two friends sent away for the Burlington Race entry forms and regulations. They hoped Carson would pattern the race after the one from London two years earlier because they knew of a seaplane that could beat its published speed. He did. Clement and Charlie registered for a race number for Keith Mitchell's Seabee.

Keith Mitchell was an aircraft maintenance engineer who worked for Genaire in St. Catharines. He had installed the cabin fuel tanks in the Aztec for Charlie and Clement's first race. Mitchell owned a Seabee, a single-engine amphibian airplane produced by Republic following World War II. In the early 1950s, Hurricane Hazel had ripped the Mitchell Seabee from its tie-downs and cartwheeled it across the St. Catharines Airport. The quiet, capable engineer completely rebuilt the airplane in his spare time over the next 20 years. He was not married and could be found working on the Seabee many evenings and most weekends. Fixing the airplane was his hobby. It was better than brand new.

Mitchell rarely flew the Seabee. When he did, it was usually with Charlie on a test flight. They never went anywhere. They just flew around to check out Mitchell's latest work. But Charlie flew it enough to know that the Seabee could be pushed beyond the maximum speed published in the aircraft's handbook.

Keith's Seabee would fly right up to the book speed with the landing gear fully retracted, but if you lowered the gear slightly, it would trail behind the wing strut and you would pick up three or four mph.

Keith was enthusiastic about John and I taking the airplane in the race, so we entered. We became Race Number 67. Keith fussed over the airplane right up to the day before the race. He fussed too much. The day before the race, the engine ran rough, too rough. We isolated the problem to the ignition on one side. I took that magneto over to Leggat's overhaul shop in Toronto and they rebuilt it while I waited. I rushed back, we put it on and the engine still ran rough. We worked through the night until we discovered that two of the ignition wires on that side had been crossed.

Charlie and Clement departed St. Catharines for Burlington at the last possible minute. They were behind on their sleep and preparations, but the airplane was running fine. It was September 11. They made a quick stop in Hamilton to top up with fuel before heading to the start at Burlington Bay.

Things did not go well right from St. Catharines. Before the race we had the Seabee's communication radio over-hauled and the compass replaced. On the way to Hamilton, the radio quit for good and all the fluid leaked out of the compass. But we had some good luck. The fuel that was being pumped at Hamilton was contaminated with water. We only took a few gallons of fuel so the water didn't affect us. Some of the other pilots had big problems.

On the first leg of the race the weather was okay, but there was a strong northwest wind blowing right on our nose. To minimize it, we flew right on the deck. It was a rough ride. We bounced along at low altitude watching for obstructions. There was no directional gyro in the airplane so we map read to save our lives to make up for the lack of compass. At times, our ground speed was only 70 knots. We had determined that our maximum time in the air at nearly full throttle was four hours and forty minutes. For a while, it looked like we might not make our first planned fuel stop in Sault Ste. Marie, Ontario.

They did make it but when they arrived at the Sault, the harbour was roughed up so badly by the wind that they had to use the lee side of a freighter to touch down. Their air time for the leg was 4:20.

The thought of a whole race-load of airplanes trying to refuel at the same floatplane dock had given Clement an idea. In the two years since his previous race, he had run for election and won a seat in the provincial legislature. John Clement, the lawyer from Niagara Falls, was now, the Honourable John Clement, Minister of Consumer and Commercial Relations for the province of Ontario.

Clement arranged with the Minister of Lands and Forests to use the government's seaplane dock at Sault Ste. Marie. When they arrived, other racing seaplanes were jockeying for position at the public dock. Charlie and Clement headed for the Lands and Forest facility where a crew from the Department of Lands and Forest was waiting to help them dock and refuel. They were out of there in 15 minutes.

They could have done it faster except for a long, slow taxi through rough water to get from the freighter to the dock and back. Water regularly broke over the nose of the airplane as it ploughed its way through the waves.

The next leg was to Thunder Bay, Ontario. Charlie and Clement followed the north shore of Lake Superior. The navigation was a lot easier, but the flight was just as slow and nearly as rough. They touched down 3:55 minutes later in the protected water of the Thunder Bay harbour. It just so happened that the Ontario Department of Lands and Forest had its own waterfront facility there with a five-man docking crew waiting for a certain Seabee.

The last leg of the day was to Kenora, Ontario. Race Number 67 followed the Trans Canada Highway which neutralized the problem of no compass. The wind dropped, the ride smoothed out and they made good time. About a half hour out of Kenora, Charlie saw that the engine oil pressure was dropping.

I looked in a rear view mirror that allows the pilot to see the landing gear position. I could see that the leading edge of the tail was covered with oil. There were plenty of lakes along the highway so I decided we would continue. When the pressure hit zero, we would land.

The pressure dropped slowly, but steadily. The Kenora Airport was the finish line. We were to fly over it and then land at Minaki Lake. We crossed over the field with the oil pressure reading 10 pounds. Normally it was 40. I landed at the airport and added oil before making the 10-minute hop over to the lake.

In the fading light at the end of a long two days, Charlie checked the engine and discovered that the oil had been coming from a pin-hole leak in the oil cooler. Fortunately for the two racers, the Minaki stop was for two nights. The next morning they flew the Seabee from the lake to a nearby dirt landing strip.

They hitched a ride into the village of Minaki and bought some tools. The oil cooler was not designed for quick-change maintenance. It took the pair all day to remove, repair and reinstall it. Charlie fixed the leak with solder and a blow torch. They ran the engine up and the repair held.

There was a banquet planned for us that night at Minaki Lodge. One of John's cabinet minister buddies was supposed to be the guest speaker. By the time we flew the Seabee back to the lake, the dinner had already started. We walked into the lodge covered in oil and headed for our room to clean up. One of the organizers intercepted us. He was all panicked because the speaker had cancelled out at the last minute. John did a quick clean up and spoke to the crowd on behalf of the Ontario government. We felt that we were paying back for the use of the Ministry's docking facilities.

The next day's race leg was to Ottawa. There was no Ministry of Lands and Forest facility along the way but Charlie and Clement had another trick up their sleeves.

Everyone they talked to was planning to refuel at Wawa, Ontario. Charlie knew there was fuel at Hawk Junction, 20 miles east of Wawa. They would be pushing their range on both legs, but with a little tail wind, they could make it. They were gambling that the extra distance would be made up with a quick stop instead of joining the crowd at Wawa.

John telephoned Hawk Air, the little air service there. The guy who answered said he would be glad to sell us fuel. John explained that we were in a race and he assured us that someone would be there.

We departed Minaki and pushed the old "Bee" to altitude to catch as much tailwind as possible. We ended up on top of broken Cumulus clouds which made navigating difficult, but we made it in four hours and 20 minutes. If there had been no one there, we would have been stranded for sure. We shouldn't have worried. As soon as we landed, a woman bolted out of a house on the hill. She ran pell mell down to the dock. As soon as we coasted in, she slapped the fuel to the Seabee without saying a word. We thanked her, paid and left.

The clouds were closer together on the second leg, but we went on top again. We had to; the leg to Ottawa was the same distance as it had been to Hawk Junction. It worked. We crossed that day's finish line at Constance Lake after four hours and 10 minutes. We planned to join the other amphibians at the Ottawa Airport to be closer to the hotel, but I wouldn't go the 20 miles without refuelling at Constance Lake.

Lady luck smiled on the pair once again at the Ottawa Airport. After nine hours of flying, Charlie shut the Seabee down on the ramp at the Ottawa Flying Club. The linecrew came over and told him he couldn't park there. He would have to move the airplane over to the grass parking. He punched the starter button and nothing happened.

Investigation proved that the brushes were burned out of the starter. It was late and there were no mechanics around. The next day was an off day for the race but it was a Saturday. There were still no mechanics, but John Bogie, owner of Laurentide Aviation, was there. He said that Charlie could use the shop facilities. Charlie found some suitable replacement brushes and with the help of Bruce McRitchie, a fellow racer and aircraft engineer from Welland, Ontario, he rebuilt the starter.

If I hadn't been asked to move the airplane, we wouldn't have discovered the problem until the Sunday race start. Then it would have been too late.

The final leg was non-stop back to Burlington. It was another low-level, into-the-wind, watch-for-obstacles, don't-get-lost leg. Two hours and 55 minutes after takeoff, Race 67 crossed the finish line of the Great Burlington Seaplane Race. The St. Catharines Seabee placed third with 580 points, five points out of first. Charlie and Clement won $2,500.

CHAPTER THIRTEEN

1975 - Helicopter

"You watch for power lines and I'll watch for cops."
                                                    Jim Maclean

𝕁im Maclean arrived at the St. Catharines Airport one day in a Bell JetRanger helicopter and called Charlie. Maclean had grown up near the Vaughn farm. Charlie had taken him for his first airplane ride when he was twelve-years-old and had taught him how to fly at the St. Catharines Flying Club. Maclean was flying helicopters for Dominion Pegasus and had stopped at St. Catharines to visit his parents on his way to Quebec City. He phoned Charlie to ask if he wanted to go along on the flight.

Everything I ever did with Jim was on the spur of the moment. I had never been in a JetRanger so I said, "Sure".

The weather was clear to start out. We flew at low level along the edge of Lake Ontario westbound to Hamilton, around the end of the lake and then eastbound past Toronto. It was a nice way to see the countryside. The visibility out of the JetRanger was superb. Jim held the helicopter at 500 feet, just off the shoreline, as we cruised along at 120 knots.

We refuelled in Kingston and checked the weather ahead. It wasn't good, but that didn't seem to bother Jim. We followed the St. Lawrence River toward Montreal until a low ceiling and steady rain forced us to fly lower. At 50 feet, Jim knew we couldn't clear the bridges in downtown Montreal. He jogged over to Highway 20 as the cloud forced us lower. We landed in a supermarket parking lot in the suburbs so Jim could use a phone booth to check the weather again. Whatever he found out seemed to satisfy him because we continued. "You watch for wires," he said calmly.

I did. I sat riveted looking straight ahead while Jim looked down. When I spotted a set of wires crossing our path, I called them out. Jim flew under most of them, but for the low ones he eased the JetRanger up into the base of the cloud, moved ahead over the wires and then dropped back down so we could see ahead again. We made it most of the way through Montreal along Sherbrooke Street but it was getting dark and foggy. Every time we ducked under wires, we tied up traffic on the street.

Finally Jim passed a police car. The officer put on his flashing lights and motioned us to land on the side of the road. I thought we were in trouble but the policeman was trying to be helpful. He told Jim to follow him to a good place to park the helicopter for the night. We flew out of town behind a police escort to a tollgate parking lot. Jim landed and the policeman gave us a ride to a nearby motel.

It was a nice gesture on the part of the cop but we had nearly made it through the worst of the weather. While we slept in the motel, the low cloud and rain moved ahead of us and the next morning we had to repeat the low level, wire-ducking run all the way to Quebec City. Jim said, "Today, you watch for power lines and I'll watch for cops."

It took us another half day of highway flying to get to Quebec City. We didn't see any policemen. We couldn't finish the last few miles in the JetRanger because the Quebec Airport sits on high ground which was in the cloud. Jim landed at a service station and we took a cab the rest of the way.

CHAPTER FOURTEEN

1978 - Ferrying

"The cockpit was dimly lit, but I could tell that he was serious about not being current."

Charlie Vaughn

August 20, 1978

The largest airplanes that Charlie had piloted carried up to 10 passengers. The longest trip he had flown was his once-in-a-lifetime air race flight from London, England, to Victoria, British Columbia.

On August 20, 1978, International ferry pilot Grant Davidson phoned and asked Charlie if he was available to fly a Hawker Siddeley HS 748 from Toronto to Jakarta, Indonesia.

Charlie had never worked for Davidson and didn't know him well. He also had never been in an HS 748, but the call sounded like a lucky break. It was Charlie's chance to crack the exclusive ferry pilot ranks. It was an offer to fly half-way around the world with an experienced ferry pilot.

Davidson was a free-lance pilot from Toronto. He was a graduate aeronautical engineer from the Royal Canadian Air Force Regular Officer Training Plan in the 1950s. He had quit the military and eventually formed his own aircraft delivery service. Charlie had met Davidson on the London to Victoria Air Race. He had flown the race in a de Havilland Turbo Beaver with his wife Jill. Since then, Charlie and Davidson had crossed paths from time to time operating in their separate aviation circles.

Charlie describes Davidson as a slim, somewhat intense man.

Ferrying aircraft was his career. He seemed driven by it.

"I've never flown an HS 748," I told Grant.

"That's okay, Charlie; you'll be flying with Glen Code. He's familiar with the airplane."

I didn't know Glen Code, but Grant had a good reputation as a ferry pilot. I assumed that his man would have the experience necessary to fly whatever an HS 748 was to Indonesia with a green-horn co-pilot. It looked like a great learning opportunity.

"Sure, Grant; I'd be glad to go. When do we leave?"

"Meet Glen at the Field Aviation hangar on Thursday morning. He's short and has a beard. I'll be leaving ahead of you in a Buffalo that I'm delivering to Abu Dhabi. I'll meet you in Abu Dhabi and take Glen's place for the rest of your trip."

"Okay."

The Hawker Siddeley HS 748 was a twin-engine turboprop made in England. It first flew in 1960 powered by two Rolls-Royce Dart engines of 2,280 horsepower each. It would carry 40 to 58 passengers and 1,440 gallons of fuel giving it a maximum takeoff weight of 46,500 pounds. The 748's would cruise at 244 knots and fly 1,720 nm without ferry tanks.

Glen Code was a Canadian Tire Store owner from Timmins, Ontario, with an interest in flying. Code did occasional flights for Austin Airways out of Timmins, including some in their HS 748s.

I called Glen and introduced myself on the phone. We discussed what arrangements he had made for the trip. I told him that I had not done much international ferry work and that I had never flown an HS 748. He didn't seem bothered by either statement. He made one suggestion. "Wear a white aircrew shirt with captain's bars on the epaulettes. It's the key to getting along with authorities overseas," he said. I thanked him and we agreed to meet on the ramp at Field Aviation early on Thursday morning.

August 23, 1978

I went to the north ramp at the Toronto International Airport looking for a short guy with a beard standing beside a big airplane with foreign military markings. I found Glen doing a walkaround on a twin-engine airliner about the size of a Vickers Vanguard. I introduced myself. Over the next week I would get to know Glen as a laid back, quiet sort of guy who was easy to work with.

He said the weather looked good and that he had filed a VFR flight plan to Goose Bay, Labrador, our first refuelling stop. Without further fuss or delay, he finished the walkaround on the airplane with me following him and climbed in. He showed me what I needed to know to work the radios and then started the engines. It was 10 o'clock.

Glen taxied out and took off. I handled the communications and set up the navigation radios. In the climbout, Glen turned on the autopilot. I wanted to learn more about the airplane, so when we reached our VFR cruising altitude, I asked Glen if I could hand-fly the airplane. He said, "Sure," so I flew all the way to Labrador without the autopilot. Four hours later, Glen took over control in the descent and landed at Goose Bay.

During the fuel stop at Goose, Code took the time to show Charlie the proper way to fill the fuel tanks on an HS 748. He told Charlie that the 748 holds seven and a half hours of fuel, but only if you know how to fill it up completely.

There are three interconnected fuel tanks in each wing. They are filled from on top. There are drip sticks under the wing that start leaking when set to a predetermined level. The trick that Glen taught me was to crack open the drip stick on the outboard tank to the full mark and then have the linecrew fill all three tanks from the outboard filler. When the drip stick starts to vent, close it and then have the linecrew slowly fill the tank to the top of the wing. That is the only way to get 7.5 hours out of a 748. The lesson proved to be invaluable to me a few days later.

Code also showed Charlie how to taxi the over-fuelled 748. If the pilot wasn't careful, the centrifugal force during a quick turn on the ground would start the fuel syphoning out the vents on one side.

The two pilots departed Goose Bay for Reykjavik, Iceland. It was 17:00 Toronto time, but they were flying against the clock. It was 18:00 in Labrador.

Glen worked the autopilot from the left seat while I worked the radios from the right. The weather was good along the way, but there was a low cloud layer covering Iceland. Glen ask me to request an IFR clearance for the approach into Reykjavik. I did and we were cleared for an ILS. Then Glen nonchalantly said, "Charlie, why don't you fly the approach?"

I told him that I didn't think it was a good idea for me to do the approach in a strange airplane in marginal weather. Then he said that he wasn't very current flying on instruments and he would really feel better if I would fly the approach and he would back me up by monitoring the airplane. In the dim light in the cockpit I could tell that this was no longer a suggestion. He was serious about not being current. I was no longer the ride-along trainee co-pilot. I took control.

The 748 is an easy airplane to fly. Fortunately, nothing went wrong to complicate the approach. The weather was above the minimums and we broke out in time to see the runway.

At Reykjavik, Charlie met Sven Bjornson again. Bjornson is every North Atlantic ferry pilot's friend. As the manager of the fixed base operation at the Reykjavik Airport, he had first met a very frozen Vaughn when Charlie was on his way to England for the air race.

Sven was a big, friendly Icelander, the kind of guy who is cheerful and helpful toward everyone no matter who they are or when they arrive. He arranged for our fuel and gave us a ride over to the hotel. By the time we got something to eat it was 10:00 pm our time; 03:00 in Iceland, which is on

Greenwich Mean Time. We had planned a long day ahead of us so we went right to bed.

August 24, 1978

This trip introduced me to the necessity for ferry pilots to sleep fast when flying against the clock. We got up at 08:00 local time and were airborne by 10:00. Our first destination was Shannon, Ireland. The weather was good all the way and the airplane was no trouble. Glen and the autopilot flew the visual approach into Ireland. Our total flight time was four hours.

We cleared customs, grabbed some food and had the airplane refuelled. By four o'clock we were headed for Ajaccio, the largest city on the French island of Corsica in the Mediterranean Sea. I flew that leg from the right seat. I was tired but I was starting to feel comfortable with the airplane. About half way into the 4.5-hour flight, three things happened about the same time. Two were expected. It got dark and we ran into cloud. The surprise was the failure of one of the right side electric fuel pumps.

According to the pilot's manual for the HS 748, a fuel pump failure was nothing to worry about, but it took the edge off the comfortable feeling I had developed for the airplane. There are two electric fuel pumps on each side and a mechanical pump in each engine. A flight can be initiated or continued with one of the electric pumps inoperative but not both on one side.

The weather was cloudy, but not stormy. We continued to Ajaccio.

Over the Mediterranean it was very black outside. I was cleared for the ILS approach, which I flew to the letter. Neither Glen nor I could see anything on the ground. The first lights we saw were the runway approach lights on short final.

Ajaccio was my first experience with an airport guarded by soldiers carrying heavy automatic weapons. At the time, there was unrest in French Morocco, so security in Corsica was tight. The soldiers didn't bother us; they just watched, but they made me nervous. I didn't like walking past armed guards in fatigues in a foreign country where I was the foreigner.

Nobody in the Ajaccio terminal building spoke English. Neither Charlie nor Code spoke French. Charlie had studied some French in high school. That had been over 30 years earlier and without enthusiasm.

I should have paid more attention.

Using gestures and one-word sentences, he tried to communicate their need for fuel and a place to stay. Eventually the airplane was filled and they were directed to a hotel across the street from the terminal building. It was midnight local time before they crawled into bed.

August 25, 1978

They were up six hours later. The morning greeted Charlie with a spectacular view of the jagged Corsican mountains that surround Ajaccio. The sight made him realize that he should have been more worried about the ILS approach the night before. The peaks were marked on the approach chart, but nothing on a piece of paper prepared Charlie for the sight of the runway laying in the bottom of a deep, narrow gorge. He had flown the ILS approach down the valley in cloud with a five-kilometre clearance between granite walls.

The next leg was to Rhodos Paradisi Airport on Rhodes, the furthest of the Greek Islands, near the border with Turkey. In Rhodos, they were supposed to meet Grant Davidson and follow him to Abu Dhabi. The plan was for Glen Code and Davidson's co-pilot to return to Canada on the airlines while Charlie and Davidson continued on to Jakarta with the HS 748.

Glen flew the leg out of Ajaccio and I worked the radios. Shortly after takeoff, we were switched to Rome Control and cleared to our requested cruising altitude of 17,000 feet. We stayed with Rome until we were past Italy and halfway across the Ionian Sea. At that point, the second electric fuel pump on the right side quit.

The aircraft manual calls for a maximum altitude of 10,000 feet when both electric pumps are unserviceable on one side. Apparently, the engine driven fuel pump will cavitate at high altitude and won't draw enough fuel to keep that engine running. I requested a descent with Rome Control. He told us to contact Athens Control. I did and asked for a lower altitude. He responded with, "Say your DME."

We didn't have any distance measuring equipment so I said, "Negative DME."

There was no answer. I waited a minute and then repeated my request for a lower altitude.

"Say your DME," the controller said.

"Negative DME," I replied. There was no response. Both engines were still running, but I didn't know for how long.

English is the official language of international air traffic control, but that does not guarantee that it is universally understood.

DME was a radio navigation aid used by most airliners. If the Athenian controller could not see Charlie's airplane on radar, it would have helped him to know the distance of the HS 748 from its destination. If he did have the airplane on his radar, then knowing 748's DME distance would still have helped him identify which aircraft was talking to him. Either way, Charlie didn't have DME equipment.

I asked for a lower altitude again.

"Say you DME!" the controller demanded.

"Negative DME," I replied. This was greeted by silence again.

"Requesting an immediate descent," I said. "Negative DME; We have no DME; there is no DME on this aircraft!"

This time the silence was broken by another pilot with an American accent who must have been flying in the area, "It figures; he has no DME."

Athens Control finally replied, "Switch to Rhodos Approach."

At this point we were getting close enough to our destination to need a descent for landing anyway. I called Rhodos and asked for a descent.

"Say your DME," the controller asked.

"Negative DME," I said. This was also greeted with silence. I couldn't believe it. I called him again and requested a descent.

"Say your DME."

"Negative DME; we have no DME; we want to descend."

Silence.

I repeated the scenario one more time. By now, we could see Rhodes Island ahead. Glen started the descent out of 17,000 and I switched to Rhodos Tower.

"Rhodos Tower, we have the airport in sight. We are descending from 17,000 feet VMC," I said.

"Go back to Rhodos Approach," the controller said. He sounded serious. I did as he requested. Glen continued the descent.

This time I told Rhodos Approach that we had an emergency and were unable to hold altitude.

"Switch to Rhodos Tower," he said.

I did and they eventually cleared us to land.

As soon as we taxied up to the ramp, the airplane was surrounded by armed soldiers. Their guns were pointed at the airplane. I was scared to death. I didn't know what to do. Glen broke the silence. "I'll take care of getting the fuel pump fixed, Charlie," he said calmly, "you see what these guys want."

I went to the door, unlatched it and swung it open. Two Greek soldiers were pointing their guns at the door. I put my hands in the air. "Take it easy fellahs," I said, giving them a nervous grin, "There are only two of us."

The head soldier motioned me toward the terminal building. I climbed down and was escorted to the air traffic control office. None of the soldiers said anything. I figured we were in big trouble for descending without a clearance.

I approached what appeared to be the supervisor in the control room. The soldiers left.

"I'm the pilot of India Hotel Bravo," I said.

"What can I do for you?" he said politely and in good English. It sounded like he knew nothing about the airplane.

"You wanted to see me?" I asked.

He scratched his head for a moment and then said, "Oh, yes. You should not descend and switch frequencies without permission."

I was feeling a lot braver without two guns at my back. "True," I replied, "but I can't land at 17,000 feet."

"Ah, yes," he said, "there is no problem." He turned to walk away.

"There is a problem!" I said. It came out louder than I expected. I was a bit high on adrenaline. "When you greet me with guns, there is a big problem."

Without knowing Charlie, it is difficult to explain why he would not have left the incident well enough alone. It is also hard to understand how Charlie gets away with making such comments, but he always does. Charlie comes across as a firm but fair person who cannot be pushed around. He has the bearing of a high school principal, a look that says he is interested in other people and willing to meet them half way. The kindness is always there, but behind it, the no-nonsense part of the man shows through. The treat-me-fair-and-I'll-treat-you-fair look about him has smoothed Charlie's way many times. It has also left him with a string of friends around the world.

"Is there anything else I can do for you?" the chief controller asked with a smile.

"Yes," I said, "we are following another airplane to Abu Dhabi. Have you heard from a de Havilland Buffalo? The pilot is Grant Davidson."

The controller stopped smiling. "Yes, he was here earlier today. We placed him under house arrest, sold him some fuel and kicked him out. He filed for Abu Dhabi and left."

"What was the problem?" I asked.

"The aircraft belonged to the Emirates Air Force. It does not make us happy to have foreign military aircraft land here without prior permission."

"I understand, thank you."

"You are welcome."

I went back outside. Glen was still in the airplane, keeping himself busy and staying out of sight. I told him what had happened to Grant.

Code and Charlie inquired at the terminal building about aircraft repair facilities for their broken fuel pumps. The same soldiers who had surrounded the 748 arranged for the mechanics at the Olympic Airways base on the airport to have a look at the airplane. The airline mechanics were not available to do the repairs, but they instructed the two pilots to remove one of the good electric pumps from the left side of the airplane and exchange it for one of the dead pumps on the right side. It took them the rest of the day and most of the night.

It wasn't much fun working in the heat of a Greek summer, sometimes up to our armpits in jet fuel, but when we were done, it worked. It was another late night by the time we got to bed.

August 26, 1978

In the morning we filed for Abu Dhabi City, the capital of the United Arab Emirates. Our route took us past the south shore of Turkey toward Lebanon. We were told to switch to Beirut Control, which we did, but there was no answer. The airway took us close enough to the Beirut Airport that we could see two MiG fighters taking off. Both Glen and I watched them with what-could-happen-next thoughts on our minds, but they peeled off in the other direction and we never saw them again. Approaching Syria, we called Damascus Control.

"India Hotel Bravo, you land Damascus," the controller said.

"No," I replied, "we are flight planned for Abu Dhabi."

"You land Damascus. I say again, you land Damascus."

He sounded pretty serious. There wasn't much cockpit debate about obeying the order after having been close to the MiGs in Lebanon. We landed at Damascus.

This time we hadn't done anything wrong. The "land or else" order was just the Syrians way of selling jet fuel and collecting a $300 airways user fee. They were friendly but firm about the fact we had to pay cash, U.S. dollars or go no further.

There was a de Havilland Buffalo with Emirates Air Force markings parked on the ramp. When we were done paying, we found Grant Davidson in the terminal building with his co-pilot.

"We were commanded to land here when we left Rhodos," Grant said with a grin. "We figured that they would do the same to you, so we decided to stay and wait. We knew you'd come along eventually."

"What if we had ignored their landing order and continued on?" I asked him.

"Their MiGs would have shot you down," he replied.

The flight from Rhodos to Damascus had only taken 2.5 hours, but it was already 11:00 am and hot. Charlie was amazed how the tension during the short flight combined with dealing with the Syrian officials in the heat of the Arab summer had sapped his strength. He and Code had thoughts of a lunch break, but Davidson had other ideas. He had been waiting for the HS 748 for a day. He was ready to have Code and Charlie follow him to Abu Dhabi.

Grant and his co-pilot climbed into the Buffalo and took off. Glen and I filed our flight plan and followed. We had snack food on the airplane, so we knew we wouldn't starve. The weather was hot but clear. This was my first time in this part of the world, so I enjoyed the view. We flew from Syria over the Nefud Desert region of Jordan and across the sandy desert region of the Arabian Peninsula.

We landed in Abu Dhabi on the shore of the Persian Gulf 5.7 hours later. It was 8:00 pm local time. Glen and I were tired and more than a little hungry. When we pulled up to the ramp, Grant was waiting. He hustled Glen off the airplane, telling him that there was still time to make the evening airline flight to London if he hurried. He did. I remember thinking that by the look of the terminal building, Abu Dhabi might be a nice clean city. I was looking forward to a good meal and a long sleep.

As soon as Glen cleared the boarding gate, Grant turned to me and asked if I was ready to go.

"Ready to go where?" I asked.

"To Bombay, India," he replied.

It was eight o'clock in the evening; I was tired and hungry; and the man was asking me if I was ready to fly across the India Ocean at night. I was the new guy on the job and I barely knew Grant. He was operating on a full day's rest, so I figured if he wanted to fly, I could ride along. I answered in the most negative affirmative that I could muster, "Sure, I'm ready if you are."

I supervised the refuelling of the HS 748 while Grant filed the flight plan. When we were ready, he came out and climbed into the right seat.

"Aren't you going to fly left seat?" I asked.

"Oh, I haven't flown one of these things in a long time. You fly left seat."

I started the airplane and taxied out. Grant worked the radios. He received our clearance and we took off. During the climbout, the controller called us back and said that we had to return and land at Abu Dhabi.

"You did not clear customs when you landed, so you must come back."

Grant looked at me and shrugged. "I'm flying the airplane," I said, "but you're making the decisions."

During our hesitation, the controller said, "If you do not return, we will impound the aircraft and jail the crew!"

Grant smiled. "I guess that settles it," he said. "Either we return so they can impound and jail us or we keep going. I vote we keep going." With that he changed frequencies.

Flying hot and tired over beautiful scenery is one thing, but flying cold and exhausted over an endless ocean in the dark is another. While Davidson dozed intermittently in the right seat, Charlie used every trick he knew to stay awake while flying down the middle of the Gulf of Oman and across the Arabian Sea south of Pakistan. He kept busy reading the charts, studying the aircraft manuals, making log entries and checking the instruments. Six hours later, they landed at Bombay. It was midnight Abu Dhabi time. It was 01:30 in India.

August 27, 1978

Charlie dragged himself off the airplane and into the terminal building. All he wanted was to sleep. The customs officer took one look at his air crew shirt, stamped his passport and waved him through. Davidson wasn't so lucky. He was dressed casually and looked a little rough around the edges. He could have easily passed for a smuggler or a terrorist. The customs officer searched him and his bag. He read Davidson's passport cover to cover and asked him a lot of questions. All this time Charlie was falling asleep on his feet on the other side of the customs counter. What he didn't realize was that Davidson had planned to do another leg.

When Grant finally got through, he said, "I'll get the airport office to stamp our flight plan. You check the weather and I'll meet you in the flight planning room."

Suddenly, I was awake. "Why, where are we going?"

"The next stop is Madras. It's just a hop across India. It's a good place to stay overnight," he replied and hustled off to the airport office.

On my own, I would have not pushed us that far, but I was still the new guy on the block. I dragged myself to the weather office.

By the time we were airborne again it was 03:30 in India. I was nearly blind with fatigue. I asked Grant if he would fly left seat, but he repeated that he wasn't very familiar with the HS 748. The "hop across India" took 2.7 hours. At least we didn't have to clear customs at Madras.

I collapsed into a cab and was ready to fall asleep when Grant told the driver where we were going to stay. The Madras Airport is well out of town. The cab driver decided that we were in a hurry. He floored the accelerator and held it there. In his mad dash to get downtown he swerved in and out of the early morning traffic. At one point he actually forced a truck to take to the sidewalk to avoid a collision.

"Slow down!" I shouted, "You're going to kill us all!"

He ignored me, so I yelled at him again to slow down. He just smiled as if he didn't understand or chose not to. By the time we reached the hotel, my shirt was soaked with sweat, I was emotionally wrecked and wide awake.

It took me nearly an hour to fall sleep. Four hours later, Grant woke me up. He was ready to go. "Charlie, those captain shirts work great. May I borrow one?" I only had two shirts with epaulettes. I gave him my only clean one.

Davidson had planned to fly from Madras to Singapore on the tip of the Malaysian Peninsula. It would be the longest leg of the trip; 1,700 nautical miles. Charlie calculated that it would take seven hours. He knew that the HS 748 was good for 7.5 hours maximum.

I told Grant that I thought we were stretching it too far. He said that it would be no problem with a little tail wind. I didn't pursue it any further, then. We headed for the weather office.

The weather office wasn't their only stop. Charlie discovered that aviation in India is badly bound by bureaucratic red tape. In order to have their flight plan accepted, the two pilots were required to have it stamped by officials at the customs, immigration, health, weather and airport offices. These were located in all different corners of the airport. Each official wore a uniform shirt with epaulettes carrying various numbers of gold stripes. The flight plan stamps were required to show that the officials in each office had given their blessing before the airplane was allowed to leave the country. Of course, these services cost money; cash; in U.S. dollars. A lot of money and too much running around later and their paperwork was considered in order.

Grant liked the shirt. "These epaulettes work pretty good," he said fingering his four stripes.

I was tired from the long day before, but I still had my sense of humour. "Don't let it go to your head," I replied. "I was just in the washroom and the guy cleaning the toilets was wearing one and his had three bars."

The weather office promised a tail wind. Singapore could be made with an hour reserve. It was mid-day and the temperature had already hit 30 degrees Celsius by the time the two pilots took off.

Now that I was somewhat rested, Grant decided to take the left seat. I worked the radios. With the heat and the fuel load, we couldn't get the HS 748 to our flight planned altitude of 19,000 feet. We levelled off at 13,000 feet. Our fuel burn was higher, our true airspeed was lower and the tailwinds were lighter. Making Singapore was going to be tight. The flight was mainly over ocean but there were a couple of airports before Singapore where we could refuel.

As we burned off the fuel load, we were able to climb slowly, but the tailwind diminished and eventually became a light headwind. Grant flew while I calculated. It looked like we would be seven hours and fifteen minutes covering the whole distance when we passed Penang, the second last available fuel stop before Singapore. We had 400 nautical miles remaining.

"We'll make it," Grant declared. "We'll gain some time and fuel in the descent."

I tried to get him to stop at Kuala Lumpur, 200 miles out, but he knew that fuel was cheaper in Singapore.

At that time, ferry pilots were paid a fixed amount to deliver an airplane. This encouraged minimum expenses to maximize profits. Buying cheaper fuel saved money and that's exactly what Davidson was doing.

Being tight on fuel at the end of a trip like that takes more out of you than the whole rest of the flight. It's easy for a ferry pilot to stop short when it's obvious there is not enough fuel, but when you have just enough plus a little bit, you go, but you sweat most of the way.

Grant was going.

When we started the descent, the little fuel that was left in the tanks moved forward off the fuel level sensors. It didn't help the tension in the cockpit to see the fuel gauges drop to zero.

I asked Singapore Approach for a straight in. He told me that there was a smaller aircraft ahead and gave us vectors for spacing.

"We are critical on fuel," I said, "I cannot accept vectors."

I expected the controller to ask questions or ignore me. He did neither. He pulled the other aircraft from the approach and cleared us for a straight in.

When we landed, we had been in the air 7.2 hours. It was a perfect Davidson delivery leg. I would have liked to have filled the tanks just to see how much it would have taken, but the next leg was only 400 nm and it was to Jakarta, our destination. Grant ordered just enough fuel to get us there.

August 28, 1978

The leg to Jakarta was uneventful but interesting. Shortly after leaving Singapore, I flew across the equator for my first time and into an aviation void. Across Indonesia, there were no navigation aids, radar or traffic. We plotted a course and flew the compass. The weather was good, except for a few mid-day cloud build-ups. We were able to map read along the eastern shore of Sumatra to Jakarta.

The two pilots landed in Jakarta after 2.7 hours. Charlie thought they might stay overnight, but not Grant Davidson. They had lunch and got on an airliner. They flew back to Singapore, on to Hong Kong, Honolulu, Los Angeles and Toronto, switching airplanes at each place but never staying for more than a couple of hours. Charlie was back home by August 30 and that included losing a day crossing the International Dateline.

The long airline ride gave me a chance to talk to Grant outside the pressure of flying an airplane on too little sleep. I came away knowing and understanding him a little better. Grant was basically a personable guy. He may have been a little overdriven to complete his trips with minimum time and expense, but he was trying to establish a career for himself in the ferry business. He was a free-spirited ferry pilot who got it done. In those days you could get away with barging across international borders without bothering with overflight clearances, so Grant did. At the end of our flight home, he asked me if I would fly with him again. I took the question as a compliment and said, "Yes."

CHAPTER FIFTEEN

1978 - Variety

"This was a busy time for me, but a good time."
Charlie Vaughn

Charlie hoped that the trip to Jakarta, Indonesia, had opened the door to international ferry flying. In the meantime, his growing reputation in Canada as a reliable pilot who could fly a variety of aircraft was providing plenty of work.

A page out of Charlie's log book during 1978 is tell-tale evidence of his ratio of farming to flying during general aviation's hey-days in the late 1970s.

Charlie worked semi-regularly for Leavens Brothers. The Toronto-based operator had an aircraft dealership and a charter department. In 1978, Charlie flew a new Cessna 337 Skymaster on a five-day eastern Canada sales demonstration tour to St. John's, Newfoundland. He worked as a copilot with Bruce Deamude on several sales demonstrations and charter trips in a Leavens' Mitsubishi MU 2 turboprop.

I also flew a Piper Navajo to LG2 and LG4, two gravel airports built in central Quebec for the James Bay Power Project. The flights were to shuttle crews and parts for Toronto-based Dominion Helicopters. They were interesting because neither airport had lights or a Non-Directional Beacon or any other ground-based navigation aids. It was a day, VFR operation only. We had to plan the trips with enough fuel to go to the airports, not get in for whatever reason and fly a long distance to an alternate.

In 1978, Charlie also flew charters in a Piper Navajo for Executive Aviation out of London, Ontario.

He continued to fly with Moe Fraser at Commander Aviation, which in 1978, acquired a Westwind 1121. When Charlie was checked out on the aircraft as a copilot, he flew it on an executive charter to Vancouver the next day.

In December of that year, Jim Plaxton, president of Dominion Helicopters, asked Charlie to train two helicopter pilots to fly the company's Navajo.

Plaxton gave me three helicopter pilots to work with on the theory that two of them would make the cut. At the time, most helicopter pilots did not have Instrument Ratings. At one point, they were all tied for last, but eventually they got the hang of it.

This was a busy time for me, but a good time. I was having fun and I was getting paid.

The Webster: In 1951, Charlie's flying instructor encouraged him to compete for the Webster Trophy. The Webster is awarded annually to Canada's top amateur pilot. Charlie placed first in the Ontario regional Webster competition and was runner-up at the nationals. Here he poses beside his own aircraft, a Piper L4-B, with the Webster Runner-up Trophy.

Specialty flying: Charlie flew a Piper J-3 Cub in a 1959 aerial pollinating experiment for a pear orchard belonging to St. Catharines farmer Garth Glass. Glass sat in the back of the airplane and operated a home-made dispersing device. He claimed it worked and named the airplane the Bumblebee.

Ag-flying: From 1954 to 1963, it was familiar to see Charlie dusting grapes in the Niagara area with Piper Cubs for Hicks and Lawrence Ltd. The larger vineyards were done with Charlie leading a three-plane formation.

Aircraft homebuilding: Charlie was one of a group of ten St. Catharines-area pilots who built CF-PEK, a Pietenpol Air Camper. As the most experienced pilot, Charlie test flew the airplane.

London to Victoria Air Race: (L-R, John Clement, Charlie Vaughn, Joe Green) St. Catharines member of parliament Joe Green christens Brights Number 74, the Piper Aztec flown by Charlie and Clement during the London to Victoria Air Race in 1971.

London to Victoria Air Race: The mountainous coast of Greenland was visible on the way to England for the London to Victoria Air Race, but was covered with low cloud and poor visibility during the actual race. Charlie has worried about these rugged peaks many times during his aircraft ferrying career.

Burlington Centennial Seaplane Race: In the summer of 1973, Charlie (left) and John Clement (right) flew Republic Seabee CF-KKK to a third-place finish in the Burlington Centennial Seaplane Race. For this race they had a few tricks up their sleeves.

CHAPTER SIXTEEN

January, 1979 - Hawaii

"There is nothing between Hawaii and California except water. I've seen it all."

Charlie Vaughn

Ⓖrant Davidson called on February 23. He talked like we were old flying buddies.

"Charlie, have you ever flown a Shorts Skyvan?" Grant asked.

He pronounced it more like a challenge than a question. It was obvious that he had a delivery flight and wanted me to go.

"No, I haven't Grant, but I've flown the same engines on the Mitsubishi MU 2."

"Well, I've never been in a Skyvan, but I've got a manual for one. Together we should be able to handle it, don't you think?"

"Handle what, Grant?"

"Hawaii. There's a Skyvan there that needs to be flown to California."

I couldn't help being caught up in his enthusiasm. I knew Skyvans were slow and that they held a lot. That's all I knew. I hoped they held a lot of fuel.

"Sure, I think so," I replied.

"Good. Meet me in Terminal One at Toronto International on February 28 at seven o'clock."

Comparing the Skyvan to an MU 2 was a bit like comparing a Cadillac to a Ryder moving van. Both vehicles have V8 engines, but you wouldn't mistake one for the other.

The Skyvan was made by Short Brothers PLC in Ireland. It can best be described as a shipping container with wings.

It is square and ugly, but functional. Two 715-hp Garrett turboprop engines pulled the 19-passenger Skyvan through the air at 150 knots. The prototype first flew in 1963. By 1979, Shorts had sold over 100 of them as military transports, commuter planes and freighters to different places around the world.

The airplane that Charlie and Davidson were going to fly had been leased to Hilo Airlines, an inter-island commuter airline in Hawaii. The lease had terminated. The airplane was going to be overhauled in California before going on lease in Gabon in western Africa. By the time the two pilots saw the airplane, the interior had been stripped out and extra fuel tanks added.

We arrived in Honolulu late on the 28th. The next morning we hopped over to Hilo Airport on Aloha Airlines where the airplane was waiting. We had planned to test fly it and then get ready to leave the following day.

Before launching across that long stretch of open ocean in a strange, well-used airplane, I would have liked to fly a short trip to test the engines, systems and fuel consumption. Since neither one of us had flown a Skyvan, I would at least have liked to do a few circuits. We couldn't do either. The airplane had already been fuelled up before we got there. Six rectangular aluminum tanks had been fitted into the cabin and filled with jet fuel. Sitting there on the ramp it weighed about 18,000 pounds, 5,500 pounds over its normal gross weight of 12,500. If we did manage to get the Skyvan airborne, it would have been too heavy to practise landings. We were going to have to takeoff in a one-shot attempt to learn the airplane, prove the systems and deliver it to California.

The ferry tank installation was very basic. The six containers were connected together without shut-off valves between them. A fuel line ran from the lead tank to two electric pumps hooked in series and then up to the regular fuel system going to the wing tanks. There was a single vent line running from an elbow in a side window to the first tank and then to the others. The plumbing was definitely hardware store variety. It was okay by Vaughn farming standards, but it was crude for an airplane that was about to be flown across the Pacific.

In order to test the ferry tank installation, we disconnected the fuel line to the wing tanks and ran it into a pail. One of the electric pumps didn't work. There was an extra one in the bag of spares along with a manual wobble pump left by the installers. I had brought some tools with me, but not enough. I had to borrow more to change the pumps.

We tried to start the airplane, but one of the two batteries was dead. We arranged a ground power unit start. The engines and systems checked out okay during a ground run-up. The radios worked on the ramp which wasn't much of a guarantee, but it was the best we could do.

Grant wanted to go early the next day.

"We can't go Grant," I said.

"Why not?"

"We need another battery. They don't put two batteries in this airplane just in case one goes flat. They are both part of the system. If we depart on a dead NiCad battery, we are risking a thermal run-a-way over the Pacific Ocean."

This was the first time I had tested my professional relationship with Grant. On our previous trip, I had been the new pilot and had gone along with his judgement on everything. Now I was questioning it.

"Charlie, it could take a week to get another battery shipped from the mainland."

"I don't care if it takes two weeks; I'm not flying this airplane on a dead battery."

We discussed it a bit more before Grant conceded that I was going to wait no matter what and so should he. We called San Francisco and ordered another battery.

As soon as Grant decided to let me have my way, he changed. He relaxed. The wait gave us time to talk about other things besides flying. I got to know Grant, the husband and father. I learned that the ferry work took him away but it provided the income for him to build a good life for his family.

The two pilots had arranged for the battery to be shipped on a Pan Am flight the next day to Honolulu and then from there to Hilo via Aloha Airlines. It didn't arrive. A call to Pan Am's Honolulu office revealed that the battery was sitting there. Aloha Airlines would not take a "wet" battery. Charlie explained their predicament to the ground agent. He said that he would take care of it and that we would get the battery the next day.

That night I got a forecast for the winds aloft in anticipation of being able to depart in the morning. In my flight planning, I had broken the route up into 300-nm segments. I used the winds to calculate the drift, speed and fuel for each leg. Grant gave me a hard time for doing all that work. "Charlie," he said, "It's North America. If we fly east, we can't miss it!"

The next morning the battery arrived on Aloha with a "Dry Battery" sticker over top of the "wet" one. We installed it and prepared to leave right away.

When we climbed on board, Grant got into the left seat and looked around. When I was settled in the right side, he said, "Since you've worked these engines before, you better fly the first leg."

I had learned from the last trip that Grant wasn't kidding when he said things like that. For my first flight in a Skyvan, I was going to be pilot-in-command.

I had already spent considerable time sitting in the cockpit on the previous day familiarizing myself with the airplane. There was no sense delaying our takeoff any longer. I pulled onto the runway, applied full power and released the brakes. The acceleration was better than I had anticipated. I held the airplane on the ground until we were well over the book rotation speed and then I eased back on the controls. I didn't expect much to happen. We still had lots of runway. The airplane lifted off right away. It didn't jump, but it did fly. We started a slow climb over the water and turned east.

I had filed for 9,000 feet. We needed that altitude to get the fuel burn for a 16-hour range. I had calculated that the flight would take 14 hours, but the wind forecast was getting old. I wanted plenty of reserve. I couldn't coax the Skyvan over 4,000 feet. Grant informed the controller. He told us that 4,000 was "inappropriate for an eastbound altitude" and we would have to descend to 3,000. Grant acknowledged but we stayed at 4,000 and reported a few minutes later that we were at 3,000.

Shortly after takeoff, the ADF quit. We didn't have any DME or Loran. This left us with two VOR receivers, which at 4,000 feet, had a range of less than 100 nm. Grant wasn't bothered, "It's North America, Charlie, fly east, we can't miss it."

I wasn't so concerned about our heading as our speed and range. The fuel consumption figures we were using had been based on Grant's Skyvan manual and my MU 2 engine book, not practical experience.

As we burned off fuel, I was able to climb slowly, but the airplane seemed to squat in level flight despite added nose-down trim. The nose-high attitude was robbing some of our speed. It was doubtful that we would make the continental U.S. coast in 16 hours.

Grant dipped the cabin tanks. The rear ones were still full. The six-tank installation was acting as one big tank. In our tail-low squat, the fuel was staying in the rear tanks. If we had continued burning the fuel from the front tanks only, the Skyvan would have eventually become more tail heavy to the point where it would have flown into a stall on its own.

I had some lock wire in my tool kit. Grant kinked the hoses that were interconnecting the tanks and used the lock wire to tie them off. Then he rigged a wobble pump in the rear tank and ran a hose to the nearly empty tank in the front. There was no autopilot, so I flew the airplane while he worked in the back. When he got everything set up, we took turns alternately hand pumping and flying. Eventually we got the airplane to fly level and then to climb to 9,000 feet. The fuel consumption came down and the speed went up. We knew we should be able to make the coast.

It was cold at 9,000 feet. We turned the heater on and discovered that it didn't work. I had a down jacket that I put on, but eventually the cold penetrated it. The only way to keep warm was to work the wobble pump.

We made course corrections every 300 nm according to my 24-hour-old wind drift calculations. We knew that we were staying roughly on track because we were able to raise airliners flying overhead. They relayed our position reports.

It was nearly 14 hours without a distance fix when Oakland Center finally asked us to "squawk ident" on our transponder. "I have you radar contact, nine miles south of Fundy Intersection."

I was proud of that. My calculations had placed us nine miles off course after flying over 1,800 nm.

"It's North America, Charlie," Grant said, "We couldn't miss it."

The last part of the flight was the hardest. We were cold and tired. The visibility dropped in the California haze and it was dark. With the help of the radar controllers, we found our way to Sacramento. Approaching the airport, Grant said, "You better fly Charlie, I've never landed one of these things."

Neither had I. The landing took all the concentration that I had left. Our total air time was 14 hours and 15 minutes.

All that I remember about the rest of that night was sitting on the edge of the bathtub in the hotel room knowing that getting into the water would be the best way to warm up, but I didn't want to because I knew it would hurt.

The next day the two pilots put just enough fuel in the Skyvan to fly it over to its destination in nearby Lodi, California. That night they took an overnight flight back to Toronto.

Despite the problems, the trip really hooked Charlie on ferry flying. His farm upbringing had taught him to make the best with what he had. That experience helped them deliver the Skyvan. He enjoyed meeting the challenges thrown at him during the trip. He looked forward to doing more work for Davidson.

August, 1979

He never saw Davidson again. In August that same year, Davidson was delivering a de Havilland Caribou from Guyana, South America, to Quebec for Air Inuit, the company that had purchased the aircraft. He was accompanied by an Air Inuit pilot and mechanic.

The Caribou is a piston-engined military transport. The sale had included spare engines and spare parts which were loaded in the cabin of the aircraft for the trip.

On the first leg, from Guyana to Barbados, Davidson ran into trouble. He managed to radio a message heard by an Air Guyana captain in another airplane. He said they were about an hour out of Barbados. One engine had failed and the other one was overheating. Davidson made it to within 50 miles of Barbados before he ditched the Caribou. Something went wrong during the ditching. All that was found was an oil slick.

CHAPTER SEVENTEEN

May 1979 - Wes McIntosh

"It helps to know the right people."
Charlie Vaughn

When Wes McIntosh retired from Transport Canada as the chief inspector of IFR standards in Ontario, he went to work for de Havilland Aircraft in Toronto flight testing and delivering aircraft. De Havilland was busy building Buffalo military transports for various governments around the world.

In May, 1979, George Neal, chief of Flight Operations at de Havilland, needed a co-pilot to help McIntosh deliver a Buffalo to Tanzania. McIntosh told him to call Charlie.

It was a big break. It had not occurred to me to apply to de Havilland for work. I had never been in a Buffalo. The trip with Grant Davidson to Jakarta in the HS 748 was my one and only flight in an aircraft as large. George Neal went on Wes's recommendation that I would be a good man for the job. Since it was a military aircraft, there was no requirement for a pilot licence endorsed on the type. George never asked to see my log book or to fill in an application form. He simply phoned me and asked if I would fly a new Buffalo to Africa with Wes. I said "Yes".

Early in the morning of May 16, I met the rest of the crew at the de Havilland factory in Downsview, north of Toronto, Ontario. John and Ben were Tanzanian Air Force pilots who would accompany us as observers. Don Chalmers was a de Havilland engineer who would make sure everything worked on the delivery. We departed that morning for St. John's, Newfoundland, with Wes doing the flying and me sitting wide-eyed in the right seat.

Wes levelled off at 11,000 and set up long-range cruise power that gave us 200 knots. He explained a few things about the Buffalo and then let me spend the rest of the first leg learning how everything else worked. It took us 5.7 hours to fly to St. John's. I thought it was a good day's flying. By the time we refuelled, it was 5:30 in St. John's. I had been awake for over 12 hours. It was a good time to have a leisurely supper and get to know the crew with easy-going Wes. But Wes told me to file a flight plan non-stop to Santa Marie in the Azores, three quarters of the way across the Atlantic. I was the new guy on this trip, so I didn't protest.

I marvelled at how these ferry pilots could keep going nearly around the clock.

I soon found Wes's answer for surviving long trips. When we were settled on course over the Atlantic, he gave me control of the airplane and nodded off to sleep. That is a good way to combat fatigue as long as you have a co-pilot who can stay awake.

I was tired so I kept myself busy learning two pieces of equipment that I had never used before: an HF communications radio that worked and a VLF Omega navigation radio. The VLF gave accurate track, distance and speed information when the right waypoints were punched in. It was a big improvement over the old "count-the-tones" Consol audio navigation. I found that the HF radio worked too well at night. When I called Gander Oceanic Control to give position reports, I was getting replies from places like Kuala Lumpur.

Occasionally one of the two Tanzanians would come forward and stand behind the pilot seats where there is a step down. The Buffalo is quiet compared to most military aircraft. We were able to talk without waking up Wes. Both Africans were interesting guys who spoke English quite well. John was over six and a half feet tall and was the more serious of the two. Ben was short and round and laughed a lot.

When we landed in the Azores, we had flown 7.2 hours, a total of 12.9 hours for the day. We had been flying against the clock which made it midnight local time.

Santa Maria was not paradise. It was a former American military base. The "hotel" was the leftover enlisted barracks. I gave Wes a hard time for pushing on to such lousy accommodations.

The next day we took off for Dakar, Senegal, on the west coast of Africa. I worked the radios from the right seat, the autopilot flew the airplane, Wes napped in the left seat and the Tanzanians alternately came forward to talk.

When I was trying to pass a position report to the Canary Islands on the HF radio, the controller said what sounded like, "Report Alpha Mike" in his Spanish-accented English. There was a lot of other communication traffic interfering with our transmissions.

I scanned the map for that part of the Atlantic but I couldn't find any waypoints labelled "Alpha Mike". I asked him to "say again".

He repeated, "Report Alpha Mike" several times. I told him that I didn't understand. He finally said, "Report on the AM radio." He had been telling me to switch to the shorter range AM band so there wouldn't be as much interference.

The flight into Dakar lasted 7.2 hours. That was enough for me. I was tired but Wes was still fresh. It was supper time, but he said the accommodation in Dakar was not great so we should keep going. Everyone else agreed, so I didn't say anything. We departed for Abidjan, Ivory Coast.

The four other crew had nodded off by the time we reached cruising altitude. The flight took us around the western bulge of Africa over exotic sounding places: Guinea, Sierra Leone and Liberia. I didn't see anything. It was dark which meant there was nothing to break the monotony. I made extra radio calls, double checked our navigation and lifted myself up and down in the seat to stay awake. It was late when we landed in Abidjan. We stayed in the Cote d'Ivoire Hotel, one of the grandest hotels in Africa, something that I didn't appreciate until I woke up the next day.

The Cote d'Ivoire was a beautiful and expensive hotel and casino. Wes said that we would be staying there another night, which was fine with me as long as I wasn't paying for it. That evening we had a long leisurely meal on the hotel patio. We started with wine and since the crew knew that I was a grape farmer from the Niagara wine country, I was designated the official taster of the group. The snobby waiter made a big production of opening the wine and pouring me a sample. I went along. I elaborately swirled the wine in the glass, held it up in the dimly lit patio and then took a mouthful. Ben was laughing the whole time.

There was a good sized beetle in the wine which was now unmistakeably in my mouth. I spit it out, spraying wine all over the patio. It was not the kind of thing seen regularly at the Cote d'Ivoire. John said in his proper English, "I have never seen anyone do that." Ben laughed.

I hastily explained to the waiter that there was a bug in his wine. He informed me that I was mistaken and proceeded to pour the wine for everyone else. He wasn't about to toss out a $40 bottle just for a bug. I insisted that the waiter bring us another bottle with the cork still in. He did, but it was probably added to our bill. I tried to find the bug on the patio, but it was too dark. Ben thought the whole production was just for his entertainment and he laughed in appreciation.

We had a good time that night. It was noon the next day before we got everyone out to the airport. We took off for Yaounde, Cameroon. Wes let me fly this leg while he worked the radios. The weather was good and I was refreshed. I enjoyed watching the changing scenery as we flew eastbound along the south shore of west Africa's belly. We passed over Ghana's white sands along the Gulf of Guinea and across the Niger River delta. It was dark by the time we were inbound for Yaounde in central Cameroon. The air traffic controller asked Wes how many people were on board the aircraft. Wes replied, "Five crew." I guess the controller thought he said, "Five two." Faced with the sudden knowledge that he had a foreign military aircraft inbound with fifty-two people on board, the controller panicked and called out the army. It was not a good situation. May 19 is Independence Day for Cameroon. The soldiers were well boozed up when they were hustled out to the airport.

When we taxied to the parking ramp, portable flood lights were turned on revealing that we were surrounded by soldiers with guns levelled at us. Wes gingerly opened the side door, but stood well back. The commanding officer came on board and asked where everyone was. We soon sorted out the mixup. The CO ordered the aircraft searched just to save face. I think they were looking for more booze to take back to their party.

We stayed overnight and had dinner in the Central Hotel in downtown Yaounde. After the meal, John and Ben excused themselves from the table. They were back in about three minutes with two hookers. Introductions were made around the table as if the girls were old friends. They weren't. Then the four of them disappeared for the night.

Our final destination was Dar es Salaam on the Indian Ocean side of Tanzania, but first we planned to stop for fuel at Tabora, in central Tanzania. We didn't need fuel, but we did need an excuse to pay a social visit to the air force colonel in Tabora who had ordered the airplane for the government.

Tabora is in Massi country, a tribe of tall African cattle herders. We were met by the colonel and his entourage. Wes presented him with rugs, a vacuum cleaner and a few other "extras". These were "gifts" ordered by the colonel during negotiations for the airplane. In return, we were invited to his house for a party. The evening started with rounds of Africoc liqueur, a white lightning that went straight to my head. This was followed by Vodka and then local wine. I drank too much and had to dive for the bathroom. The Africans drank twice as much as I did. By my experience, they should have been dead, but it didn't seem to affect them too much.

Later the next morning, we flew over to Dar es Salaam, a port city which is the jumping off point for people climbing Mount Kilimanjaro. The weather was good and the scenery was spectacular but it was wasted on me. I had a pounding headache and didn't pay attention to much other than the airplane.

We handed the Buffalo over to the Tanzanian Air Force in a small ceremony. I refused all offers of refreshment. Wes and I said our goodbyes to John and Ben and booked into the Bahari Beach Hotel, north of downtown. We had tickets on a morning flight out to London on British Airways.

That evening, Wes and I planned a quiet dinner in the hotel, but a group of British Airways flight and cabin crew were having a birthday celebration for one of their own at the next table. We joined them for awhile but retired on the excuse that we had an early flight out the next morning.

When we boarded the British Airways VC-10, we recognized the crew. They were the same ones having the party. The captain invited me up front during the flight. I had been in the cockpit of an airliner before, but just for short visits. I always imagined that airline pilots worked in a sterile environment with strict rules and procedures. They didn't. When we were approaching Addis Ababa in Ethiopia, it was very hazy. The captain was flying and looking out the window trying to avoid doing an ILS approach. He said, "I think the airport is over here." The co-pilot disagreed, "I think it's over there." The co-pilot won. The captain cranked the jetliner into a bank to make the landing.

When I sat with Wes later, I told him that the crew flew just like we did.

CHAPTER EIGHTEEN

September, 1979
Buffalos to the Middle East

"In that part of the world, the air traffic controllers all talk as if they're mad at you."

Charlie Vaughn

At the end of August, 1979 Wes McIntosh called and asked me to deliver a new Buffalo with him to Abu Dhabi, the capital of the United Arab Emirates. We flew a marathon 12 hours the first day: four and a half hours from Toronto to Goose Bay, Labrador, and then seven and a half hours over the Davis Strait, across Greenland to Reykjavik, Iceland. I was looking forward to the spectacular mountain scenery of Greenland but it was too late in the day and the sun had set.

The marathon part didn't bother me too much. The Buffalo is a great airplane to fly. It has bags of extra horsepower, making it easy to take off and climb and the autopilot works well. I took my Loran receiver with me. The cabin carried a quantity of spare parts that were part of the sale, but the airplane was under its maximum gross weight and performed well. Wes nodded off regularly during the flight, but with the autopilot I just had to monitor the Loran and the airplane. We landed at Reykjavik at ten o'clock in the evening Toronto time. It was 3:00 am local time in Iceland.

Wes was up bright and early and ready to go the next morning. I met the fixed base operator, Sven Bjorson, at the airport again on our way out. He was friendly and helpful, as always.

Wes planned the next leg to Shoreham on the west coast of England near Brighton. I had never heard of it and couldn't find it on my IFR charts. It turned out to be a grass airstrip.

The short turf runway was no problem for the Buffalo but it hardly seemed like a typical stopover for an international ferry flight. Wes explained the reason we were going to land there was Ben Gunn. Gunn was the airport manager at Shoreham. Wes had met him on some other trip. The two men had hit it off well, so every Buffalo delivery with Wes included a stop at Shoreham. Wes dropped the Buffalo into Shoreham's grass runway with no trouble.

I met Ben and had to agree that he was a real character in the true sense of the word. He was one of the few people who could out talk Wes. We had only flown 5.7 hours to get there, but it had become a ritual for Wes to stay overnight at Shoreham.

The next day we departed for Kerkira on the island of Corfu off the west coast of Greece. We flew over the south of England, crossed the English Channel, across France, Switzerland and down the full length of the Adriatic Sea separating Italy and Yugoslavia.

It was a tough flight. There were thunderstorms all over Europe. The turbulence was horrendous. The engineer accompanying us had to go back in the cabin more than once to check the lashings on the boxes of spare parts. We were on the radio constantly either asking for vectors around the storms or receiving vectors around the rest of Europe's traffic. There was no napping for Wes.

We had been flying seven hours before we started our descent into Corfu. When we were switched to Kerkira Tower, the controller said that the airport was closing for the night and asked us to state our intentions. Wes told him that we would like to land. It didn't do any good. In that part of the world, the air traffic controllers all talk as if they are mad at you. They sound loud and excited all the time. Part of the problem is their difficulty with English, but an irritated attitude also comes through. As far as the Kerkira controller was concerned, the airport was closed and that was all there was to it. It didn't matter that we had flown all the way across Europe and were only 20 minutes late. We diverted to Athens.

We didn't take any time to tour Athens, but at least going to and from our hotel overnight, I got my first look at Greece.

In the morning the ground controller was just as unfriendly as the one at Corfu. At nine o'clock in the morning it was already 30 degrees Celsius outside and hotter in the cockpit. Wes called for a start-up clearance for a flight to Luxor, Egypt. The controller yelled at him. We apparently needed a time to call for a start-up clearance and then we could call back at that time, not before and not after. Wes obeyed and we sat sweating in the cockpit at least 20 minutes until it was the appropriate time to call for a start-up clearance.

We flew across the Mediterranean Sea to Cairo and then up the Nile River Valley to Luxor. There I learned about ducking bribe payments. All the officials at Luxor wanted handouts, but it isn't necessary to pay them. We had stayed ahead of our scheduled delivery time in Abu Dhabi. Now we had to wait for two days for the schedule to catch up to us. Since we weren't in a hurry, we out waited the officials who fumbled with our documents in an effort to secure a pay off. That doesn't work if you are in a rush.

We spent the two days touring some of the ancient ruins in Luxor and in nearby Thebes.

On September 3, we flew five hours to Bahrain in the Persian Gulf. We waited to adjust our timing to arrive at Abu Dhabi exactly on schedule that afternoon. There were top ranking United Arab Emirates Air Force officials who were waiting at a certain time to accept delivery of the airplane. It was interesting to be part of the ceremonies. I hoped to fly more new airplane deliveries.

Fly he did. Over the next three years Charlie would deliver more Buffalos, usually with Wes McIntosh and always with a landing at Shoreham's grass strip. In 1980, the UAE Air Force officials decided they wanted a special radio package in their Buffalos. They made a deal with Navair, a radio installation shop in Toronto, to design and install the package. Navair planned to install the radios in Abu Dhabi, but first they needed a UAE Buffalo in Toronto to design the package. Wes McIntosh and Charlie flew the airplane both ways.

The Egyptian Air Force also ordered new Buffalos. Charlie helped deliver them including being part of the crew on a three-plane group delivery to Cairo in March of 1982.

After that flight, the Egyptians decided they could deliver the Buffalos on their own. In June, 1982, I was asked to fly with de Havilland pilot Bill Loverseed and five Egyptian Air Force pilots on a delivery to Cairo. The idea was to train the Egyptians on the art of international ferrying.

It didn't work. Bill and I knew it wouldn't. We had been exposed to Egyptian pilots before. We knew that they could fly the airplanes but they had no concept of IFR rules, procedures or navigation. As long as they could see the ground and it was Egypt, they were okay, but one ferry flight from Toronto was not going to improve on that.

We started out with Bill and I flying in the pilot seats and the Egyptians taking turns standing between us and watching. We explained what we were doing. They nodded and smiled a lot. After a full day of this to Reykjavik, Iceland, they were itching to trade places with us. We held them off by explaining that our next two legs were to London, England, and then across Europe where the procedures were very complicated. It wasn't a lie. The European procedures were beyond anything the Egyptians had experienced. Bill promised them the pilot seats after Europe. I didn't know how he was going to manage that without getting us lost, killed or both.

We stopped for fuel at Iraklion, Crete. Bill installed General Ansari, the senior pilot in the left seat and one of the other Egyptians in the right. He turned to me and said, "You stand between them Charlie and help them find Egypt." Then he walked to the back of the airplane and sat down.

The first thing they did was call for an IFR clearance. The Greek controller yelled it back to them in rapid-fire broken English. Neither pilot copied anything down. They both turned to me with lost looks on their faces. I reached over, picked up the hand-held microphone and read the clearance back from memory. It's not hard to do when you understand the system, file the flight plan yourself and have done it many times before.

The two pilots got us airborne okay, but they did nothing to set up the navigation radios. I did it for them. They flew the VOR needle like it was an ADF. They turned toward the needle expecting it to move. When it didn't, they continued in a circle. The radar controller yelled at them. I got them straightened out.

Hands and feet wise, they could fly the airplane. Once we were under Egyptian control, they seemed okay talking in Arabic. They were even on track with the VOR. I went and sat down for half an hour. When I went back, I saw that one of them had switched the active VOR frequency by mistake. The VOR indicator showed "off", but that left the needle centred. They were happily thinking the airplane was on course, but it wasn't. They had changed direction and we were headed out over the desert somewhere. I got them turned around headed for our destination, the Almaza Air Force Base. They landed all right and thanked me profusely for the trip. General Asari told me that anytime I was in Egypt, I should use his name. I guess he knew I would be visiting again to deliver Buffalos. They never delivered one on their own.

CHAPTER NINETEEN

February, 1980
Around the world

*"Be gone," the controller said. "If you stay, I'll be in
trouble and you'll be worse."*

𝕱loyd Carson called Charlie and asked him if he would
deliver a Hawker Siddeley 748 from Singapore to Toronto.
Carson was the Burlington, Ontario-based aircraft broker
who had flown in the London to Victoria Air Race and had
organized the Burlington Centennial Seaplane Race. He knew
Charlie well but this was the first time he had asked him to
do an international delivery.

Carson told Charlie that he would be flying to Singapore
to see the deal completed, but would not be flying back on the
748. He asked if Charlie knew another pilot who could
complete the crew. Charlie had only flown an HS 748 once,
but felt confident about doing the trip with an experienced
international ferry pilot. He called Wes McIntosh. McIntosh
said he was available and happy to go. Then he said he had
never flown a 748 before. It would be a bit like the blind
leading the deaf, but they decided to do it.

The three of us met in Toronto on February 10, 1980. I
filled in a type endorsement for an HS 748 on Wes's pilot
licence and signed it as if I was a qualified Canadian
inspector. This was in case the officials in Singapore
asked for it.

We flew to Calgary, Alberta, in a Lear 24. Floyd was
delivering it to a customer in Calgary. I had never been in a
Learjet before. Floyd let me ride up front for some flying time
that led to a type endorsement later on.

That same day we hopped airliners that took us from Calgary to Vancouver to Los Angeles to Hong Kong and on to Singapore. We didn't stay overnight anywhere along the way. I dozed off occasionally but I don't sleep well in airplanes and I was dead tired when we arrived in Singapore. We met Carson's agent Dan Cooley who immediately took us out for a night on the town. We had dinner at the Raffles Hotel. Wes fell asleep in his chair before the meal was served. Then Dan insisted that we go to the American Club for drinks and a little gambling. Later, we crawled into a bed for the first time in 48 hours.

The next day and a half were used to catch up on sleep and test fly the aircraft while we waited for overflight clearances for our route. The engines ran fine and the radios worked. It looked like it was going to be a good trip. Floyd spent the time rounding up some teak planks. A friend of his in Toronto was building a wooden boat and Floyd had promised to bring him back teak from this trip. The planks where laid on the floor of the 748. I asked Floyd how he thought we were going to get the wood through Canadian customs. "If they give you a hard time," he said with a laugh, "tell them you needed the planks for a life raft in case you had to ditch in the ocean."

Singapore is a clean and beautiful city to visit. Wes and I managed some sightseeing. In the newer parts, the wide avenues are lined with flowers. Wes looked out of place. He had decided to grow a beard on this trip. Between the chin stubble and his rumpled jeans, he looked more like a bum than a pilot. I stayed clean cut and neat in my captain's shirts. Wes was the experienced international delivery pilot so I didn't say anything about his appearance. I should have.

As the leading expert on the 748, I flew from the left seat. We agreed that I would supervise the refuellings while Wes took care of the flight plans during the stopovers for gas. We departed for the resort island of Phucket just before midnight on February 13. It was a 3.3-hour flight in good weather up the west side of the Malaysian Peninsula. At Phucket, I used Glen Code's refuelling trick to get the maximum fuel into the 748. We were planning to make Madras on the east coast of

India in one hop. It would take most of the 748's range. Wes disappeared inside the terminal building with our next flight plan and didn't come out. When the refuelling was done, I went inside to see what had happened to him. The police had taken him into custody. They decided that he looked like a terrorist, a drug dealer or a beggar and they didn't want to take any chances. The language barrier prevented him from convincing them otherwise. They recognized me as the captain of the aircraft. Using my limited French and some English, I was able to talk them into releasing him into my custody. I told them that I would keep a close eye on him.

Wes figured Madras would take 6.5 hours flying time. We had 7.5 hours fuel at best. There was no suitable alternate airport near Madras, so we needed the good weather that was forecast and headwinds no stronger than predicted. We also needed the Indian radio navigation aids to be working. The flight would be over water for 99 per cent of the route, straight across the Bay of Bengal. With GPS, a tight leg like that would be no problem. If you didn't get the needed ground speed early in the trip, you could turn back. In 1980, there was no GPS. In that part of the world, there was no Loran or radar coverage either. We had one navigation fix enroute, the non-directional beacon on Nicobar Island about one third of the way across the Bay of Bengal.

We took off and headed west. Two hours of ocean later, we caught the NDB signal. We were on course. The island came into view about 50 miles ahead from 16,000 feet. We knew we should be able to make it all the way. Five and a half hours after takeoff, our VOR receiver picked up Madras. We started the descent into the afternoon haze and heat along the Indian coast, found the airport and landed. Our total time enroute was six hours and 20 minutes. There is a lot of satisfaction derived from planning and executing a tricky flight like that.

We were tired and hungry from having flown all night and a good part of the day. It was incredibly hot. Our shirts were soaking wet before we got out of the airplane. The Indian customs and airport arrival procedures took an extra long time.

Once we were clear of the terminal building, we went looking for a good meal and a hot bath. The restaurant we picked had no beer and the menu was in Hindi. I just pointed at something. The waiter said, "Oh no, too hot for you, sir!" I told him to bring me anything. I don't know what I picked originally, but whatever I got nearly burned my face off.

The next morning we departed for Bombay. The refuelling turnaround there took four hours. The only thing dependable in India is that nothing is dependable. The Bombay air traffic controller refused us permission to take off because the airport control needed two more copies of our general declaration form. We had to taxi back in and find a copier in the terminal building to comply with their request.

Charlie had applied for overflight clearances along their route by Telex from Singapore. Not all of the needed confirmations came back before he left but Grant Davidson had taught him to press on regardless. He knew it could take forever to receive all of the necessary paperwork for an international flight in that area of the world.

The flight from Bombay across the Arabian Sea to Muscat, Oman, on the tip of the Arabian Peninsula was no problem. The weather was clear and the wind was light. We landed in the evening after five hours in the air. We should have stopped overnight, but I wanted to stick to our original plan for one more leg that day to Riyadh, the capital of Saudi Arabia. Otherwise I would have to reapply for several overflight clearances. We pressed on.

Our flight path followed the Persian Gulf along the coast of the United Arab Emirates, past Qatar and Bahrain. We didn't see much since it was dark. The only thing that kept me awake was my hunger. We had not had a meal since the curried mystery on the other side of India.

The Bahrain controller told us that we didn't have an overflight clearance for Saudi Arabia or prior permission to land at Riyadh. He was right. I had applied for them, but I didn't have them. I told him that the approvals should be on file and asked him to track them down. He said he would see what he could do. He gave us a holding clearance over a beacon in the desert.

I was just about to give up on getting into Saudi Arabia and fly back to Bahrain when the controller said he had found a record of our clearances. We continued to Riyadh. When I called the Riyadh controller, he said that we didn't have landing permission. I told him that we did. I was tired, hungry and undiplomatic. He said we needed written permission to land. I told him that I had applied for permission and if he needed it in writing, he could get it for me. I also told him that we were low on fuel which wasn't true, but it would have been if we had been required to fly to somewhere else. He cleared us to land.

When we taxied to the ramp, the controller told me to contact him when I got into the terminal building. I left Wes to supervise the refuelling and called the controller on the telephone. We repeated our conversation about prior written permission. The bottom line was that we had to depart as soon as we had refuelled. There would be no overnight in Riyadh. "Be gone," the controller said. "If you stay, I'll be in trouble and you'll be worse."

There was no food available in the terminal building. Wes and I climbed back into the 748 with our eyes at half mast and our stomachs knocking against our backbones. During our start check, I could see that the fuel on the left side was only two thirds full. Wes had dropped the wrong dip stick. The outboard tank on that side was empty. I decided to continue because I was too tired to face the prospect of explaining why we were not leaving right away as ordered. We were headed for Luxor which was five hours away, well within our reduced range.

This decision started a chain of events that could have easily led to the tired pilots running out of gas. Charlie knew he could cross feed some fuel from the right side tanks to correct the weight imbalance. What he didn't know was that the crossfeed valve was leaking fuel when it was selected. Some fuel from the right side was being transferred, but most of it was leaking into the belly of the airplane.

It was the middle of the night local time when they departed Riyadh, but they had been up for 24 hours Madras time. On departure they were cleared directly over Medina, the city which leads to Mecca. This is normally forbidden. The two pilots didn't know it, but the direct routing saved their night. It shortened the route enough that the leaking fuel did not become a big problem. But they had not seen the last of their troubles.

Both of our radio transmitters quit over the Red Sea. I couldn't raise the controller at Luxor, but I could hear him. The fact that both transmitters quit at once indicated that their problems were related, but I was too tired and couldn't figure it out. I continued flying inbound. When I had the airport in sight in the early morning light, I lowered the landing gear and turned on all my lights. The controller saw us. "If you read me," he said, "do a 360 degree turn." I flew a circle and he cleared us to land.

When we climbed out of the airplane, I could see fuel dripping out of every nook and cranny of the belly and there was significant oil leaking out of the left engine. I was so tired and hungry that the sight of all this was like having a huge weight dropped on me. I was suddenly very depressed. The smiling ramp handler ran over with his chocks in hand and in heavily accented English said, "Oh Captain Charlie, welcome to Luxor!"

The two pilots ate and went to bed that afternoon. They slept right through the rest of the day and the night.

Luxor did not have much for aircraft maintenance facilities. Charlie worked on the snags himself. The radio problem turned out to be a stuck relay in the number one transmitter. It blocked the use of the number two transmitter. With the number one turned off, the other one worked fine, but the batteries went flat while he was doing this troubleshooting.

The batteries were pretty well shot, but I knew we would wait a long time for replacements. I borrowed a charger from the Egypt Air base on the airport and put the batteries on it before we went to the hotel that night.

When I went looking for the fuel leaks, I found a broken joint at the crossfeed valve. I was able to patch it by clamping a piece of rubber hose over the line. The engine oil leak I couldn't fix, but I decided it was small enough that I could get away with just adding oil. The local Egypt Air agent phoned his base in Cairo and ordered oil for me. It arrived that afternoon accompanied by two "mechanics" to install it and a bill for $600. I asked the one who seemed to understand English if he knew the 748.

"Oh, yes," he said, "Very much."

I made the mistake of doing something else rather than watching him. He overfilled the engine with oil. I managed to get some of the excess out, but not all.

The next morning we were somewhat refreshed and more or less ready to go. There was a ground power unit at Luxor, but it was Russian and its plug did not fit the 748. I hoped the old batteries were charged up enough to give us one more start. They were.

We took off and flew northbound down the Nile River Valley and across the Mediterranean to Iraklion, Greece. There we managed to scrounge more engine oil from Olympic Airways to stay ahead of the engine leak. There was only a little bit of fuel dripping from the crossfeed line in the belly so we refuelled and continued with a GPU start. From there we flew northwest across the Agean Sea to Nice, Italy, where we stayed overnight. It was a ten-hour flying day with no new major snags. Things were looking up.

From Nice, Charlie and McIntosh flew over the Alps and across Europe to Shannon, Ireland, in five hours and then half way across the North Atlantic to Reykjavik, Iceland, in 4.2 hours for their next overnight. The following day they flew into a large area of high pressure that held good weather and cold air. The two pilots had flown from plus 40 degrees Celsius in Luxor, Egypt, to minus 40 degrees approaching Greenland in two and a half days.

By the time we landed at Sondre Strom, Greenland, bubbles were appearing in all of the cockpit windows. The multiple layers were delaminating. The intense cold was too much for the tropic-aged panes. From then on, we should have flown unpressurized below 10,000 feet, but the fuel consumption at that level was too high and the airspeed too low to make Goose Bay, Labrador. The windows were still solidly in place, they were just full of bubbles. We decided to fly pressurized and to see if the windows got worse. They did, but only a little bit. Some of the little bubbles joined up to make big bubbles but I don't think we were in danger of the windows popping in or out. It was difficult to enjoy the scenery. Now I think I know how a grasshopper feels after a hard day of navigating through multi-faceted eyes.

The two pilots landed at Goose Bay at supper time. They could have stayed overnight, but the weather was good. They had been on the road a long time and were anxious to get home. A check of the fuel and oil leaks indicated that they were only getting a little worse so they departed for Toronto.

Six hours later, they landed at Toronto International Airport at two o'clock in the morning. The left engine nacelle was bathed in oil, fuel streaks extended from the belly to the tip of the tail, but they were home.

It had been a long, tough trip. We were happy to have made it. We were also a little punchy from fatigue. When the customs officer inspected the airplane, he asked what the teak planks were for. Wes and I looked at each other. "That's our life raft," Wes told him, "in case we were forced down in the ocean."

"Oh, good idea."

CHAPTER TWENTY

1981 - Ghana again, again and again

"Charlie is the best. He is so resourceful. When you ask him to deliver an airplane, you know he won't abandon it at the first sign of trouble, as some other pilots would."

Floyd Carson

𝕴n February of 1981, Charlie travelled to Accra, Ghana, in west Africa with Glen Code to pick up another Hawker Siddeley HS 748 for aircraft sales broker Floyd Carson. It was a Ghana Airways airplane that Carson had sold to Eastern Provincial Airways in St. John's, Newfoundland.

We flew British Airways to London and then to Accra. Ghana Airways arranged for us to be met at the terminal building. A young Ghanian walked up to me as we stepped off the plane, "Captain Vaughn?" he asked. I was impressed. I had never been in the country before.

"How did this guy know me?" I said to Glen.

"Look around you, Charlie," he replied. The terminal building was filled with Africans. We were the only white men in sight. "He had a fifty/fifty chance of being right."

The customs agents wanted to search us, which was bad news. We were both carrying a large amount of American cash for fuel purchases during the delivery. "No search," I said, pointing to the epaulettes on my shirt, "We are flight crew, Ghana Airways."

The customs agent looked at our escort who nodded in agreement. They let us go.

Eastern Provincial Airways had sent mechanics Roy Freak and Glen Hefford ahead to check over the airplane. Code and Charlie ran the airplane up on the ramp and found that everything was working. They just needed the export release papers from the Ghana government before they could depart.

The airplane was not going to be released until the Africans had the money for it, but Carson knew better than to hand over the money and expect an airplane in return. He arranged for a letter of credit to be placed with a bank of their choice in London, England.

It was a no go. The problem was, the Ghanian government officials liked to get their fingers in the pie. The letter of credit in England made that difficult. Floyd paid Aboadjie Mensah, one of the local Ashanti tribe chiefs, to act as a facilitator. They negotiated back and forth for two weeks. In the meantime, Floyd was paying Glen and me to cool our heels in the hotel downtown. He was hoping to spring the deal soon. EPA needed the airplane badly. Every day was costing them lost revenue.

I enjoyed being in a strange country but we couldn't stray too far from Accra, in case the deal closed. When it did, Floyd wanted us to leave right away. Accra was a large metropolis with colourful markets but there wasn't too much to see or do. Ghana was a contrast of wealth and poverty. The country was poorly run. The telephones didn't work very well. It was impossible to make an overseas call home.

After two weeks, Carson sent Code and Charlie home. Then he flew to England for a couple of days to make phone calls and to talk to his bank. He went back to Africa and arranged with the Bank of Ghana for the money to be placed in the bank's name in London.

Aboadjie was furious that Floyd had done something without his facilitating. Floyd said that Aboadjie had threatened to cut him up into little pieces. This was a guy that he was paying to help! It took another week for Floyd to get close to making a deal on the airplane.

Floyd went back to England and called me. We decided that I would come over on my own. Floyd would be my copilot if we managed to spring the airplane.

I arrived in Accra for the second time. Carson thought he had a deal, but every time they were ready to release the money in exchange for the export permits, there would be an unexplained delay. While waiting, I talked to the two mechanics from Eastern Provincial Airlines. They had remained in Africa the whole time. They found the delays frustrating. They knew how much their airline needed the airplane. I found out that they had been handing out small bribes to the locals at the airport hoping to speed things along. They didn't realize that their little handouts had the opposite effect. The Africans knew that the money would stop as soon as the airplane was released. The 748 was doomed to stay in Ghana. We put a stop to the bribes, but Floyd agreed that it would be awhile before anything happened. I flew home again and Floyd went to London to make more phone calls.

It was April. Carson had spent over a month of trips to London and back before he had negotiated a method of payment and release agreeable to both sides. He called Charlie and asked him to come to Ghana again. Chester Walker, chief pilot and vice-president of Eastern Provincial Airlines, also went to Ghana to be Charlie's copilot. He hoped his presence would help things along.

Chester was a nice guy, but he was anxious to get this airplane. When we met in Accra, I asked him if he had an endorsement on the HS 748. He said "No, I've never flown one, but if you can fly it, I'll go with you."

I was concerned that the Ghanians would use his lack of endorsement to delay us again. I added an HS 748 endorsement to his pilot licence with the hotel typewriter. I signed it as the testing inspector and then smudged it to make it look old.

Despite promises, the airplane was still not released. Carson turned to the friends he had made in the Ghanian business community. He had met Salima Calmoney on a flight from London. She was one of several powerful women in business in Accra. Salima owned a bus company in Ghana. Carson told her about the difficulties getting the airplane released. She arranged a cocktail party in her house and invited the five Canadians who were waiting for the airplane. She said there would be people there who could help them.

When Carson arrived at the party, there was a large crowd of well-dressed Africans. Salima pointed to a gentleman in the corner and told Carson to speak to him about the trouble with the airplane release. He did. It turned out the man was a judge in the Ghana Supreme Court. He listened and then gave Carson the name of the head of security for Ghana and told him to see him the next day.

The security chief told Carson, "You can call your crew together and go with the airplane."

"When," Carson asked.

"Right now if you want."

Carson called Charlie and Chester and met them at the airport. Sure enough, the airplane had been released, but there was still a hitch. The airport officials said the airplane had to be test flown to meet the Civil Aviation requirements. Then they handed Charlie a huge British Certificate of Airworthiness test flight form. They wanted him to fly the battery of tests listed on the form and return the report.

The complete Certificate of Airworthiness testing would have taken a couple of days. Johnny Tando, the director of maintenance for Ghana Airways, came to our rescue. He gave me a copy of a previous CAA test flight form done on an HS 748. I copied the numbers onto the new form, then Chester and I went flying. We planned to do a one-hour sightseeing flight around the area and then hand in the form. When we rotated on takeoff, most of the cockpit annunciator lights came on. When we sorted them out in the climb, we discovered that both generators had shut down. We continued the flight without them, but we knew we couldn't fly very far like that.

When we got out of the airplane at the end of the flight, there was fuel leaking out of the wings. The Ghanian officials accepted the paper work and said they would have the fuel leaks and generators fixed. By that night, everything was supposedly done so we started to load the spare parts that came with the deal. We planned to leave the next day. One of the spares was an HS 748 engine. Watching the Ghanians trying to load the engine through the passenger door was both funny and painful. They didn't have proper loading equipment and were having all kinds of trouble. It looked like they would drop the whole thing on the ramp, so we told them to leave it. Floyd planned to stay and arrange shipping for what spares could not be easily loaded.

We took off first thing in the morning. It was May 1, nearly three months from the first time I had tried to fly the airplane out.

As soon as we rotated on the runway, both generators quit. I managed to get them back on line by recycling their switches.

We climbed northwest across Ivory Coast. Our first planned fuel stop was Dakar, Senegal, about six hours away. That distance should not have been a problem except the cabin wouldn't hold pressure. We were forced to fly below 13,000 feet which gave us a slower airspeed and significantly increased our fuel consumption. We calculated that we would still make it with about 30 minutes of fuel to spare, depending on how much was still leaking. To land sooner meant taking the long way around the curvature of the west African coast and stopping at a country for which we had no prearranged fuel or customs. I wanted to go to Dakar because I knew that Air Senegal operated HS 748s. We pressed on and made it, six hours and fifteen minutes later. There wasn't much fuel left.

We had originally planned just to stop for fuel, but I asked Air Senegal to have a mechanic check our pressurization problem. They sent a nice, young African who started by looking at the circuit breakers. Drawing on my limited

French, I explained to him that the pressure system had nothing to do with the circuit breakers. He seemed to understand. Then he asked us to run one engine so he could try the pressure system on the ground. I knew that a landing gear squat switch prevented ground pressurization. Besides, two windows and a door were open. I told him to forget it. He left and came back with a bill for $600 U.S. When I protested, he just shrugged. I went to the Air Senegal maintenance office with him and talked his supervisor down to $250.

We departed for Las Palmas in the Canary Islands where we planned to stay overnight. The same problem with the generators and pressurization occurred on takeoff. The next morning, we took some time to add tape to the door seals and emergency exits on the theory that the pressure system was blowing past the old seals.

It didn't help. During our next leg to Santiago, Spain, there was still no pressure. Even though it was after five o'clock when we landed in Spain, we decided to press on to Shannon, Ireland. I went into the terminal building for flight planning and left Chester to supervise the refuelling.

He came running into the flight planning office. "You'd better come and see this," he said.

I went back out with him. There was fuel all over the place. The refuellers had been anxious to go home and had run up the pressure on the fuel feed system. The extra force blew a seal on a valve. There was kerosene pouring out all along the trailing edge and root of the wing and running across the ramp. Eventually, the outflow slowed to drips, but it was impossible to tell where the leaks were coming from. The airport firemen arrived and hosed the excess off the ramp into the drains. The refuellers were still anxious to go home and insisted on being paid cash in the local currency. I went to the terminal building to change some American dollars into Pesados while Chester telephoned the Eastern Provincial maintenance base in Gander for advice.

Gander told us that the blown valve would be no problem as long the airplane was gravity fuelled from on top of the wings for the rest of the trip. I checked the drip sticks and saw that the fuel tanks were full. I hand cranked the flaps down and opened some wing panels to drain some of the trapped fuel. We cleaned up the loose fuel along the trailing edge with rags as best we could.

On the flight to Shannon, we encountered some icing in cloud as we flew north. None of the de-icing boots held pressure. They were all rotten from too many years in the African sun. The airplane carried the ice without any problem and we landed at Shannon after midnight.

During this leg, Chester sounded me out about getting Floyd to fill in as co-pilot from Shannon so he could join his wife in Spain. She was there on holidays, a vacation they had planned before all the delays with getting the 748 delivered. When we landed at Shannon, I telephoned Floyd at his hotel in London.

When Charlie called, it was two o'clock in the morning. Carson had never flown a 748 before, but he agreed to take the next flight to Shannon in the morning. Walker headed to Spain.

While Charlie waited for Carson to join him, he dug out the maintenance manuals for the 748 that were among the spare parts. A trouble shooting procedure for the cabin pressurization led him to a ditching handle in the cockpit. The multi-function lever included a dump valve for the cabin pressure.

I discovered that a connecting spring on the pressure dump valve was overextended, which prevented the valve from closing. I fixed that and hoped that the cabin pressure would work.

Floyd arrived in the middle of the afternoon. I was mopping up fuel that had pooled under the cabin floor. We decided on a departure early the next morning. I filed two flight plans, one for Reykjavik, Iceland, and one for Manchester, England. If the pressure system worked, we would fly west; if not, we would fly to a Hawker Siddeley maintenance base at Manchester.

I took Floyd to Durty Nelles pub for dinner that night. The owner greeted me like an old friend and introduced us to a group of seven or eight of his buddies who were having a roaring good time at one of the tables. It was a Sunday and they explained that at church that morning, the topic had been the evils of drink. "So we thought we should come and investigate for ourselves," they said with a laugh.

We joined them and one asked my occupation. "Right now," I said, "I'm a pilot."

"You don't look like a pilot," he replied.

"What do I look like?" I asked.

"A farmer," he said.

When they rotated off the runway the next morning, every caution lamp in the airplane lit up the cockpit like a Christmas tree. Charlie ignored them all and continued into the climb, but it scared his new copilot.

"Holy Christ, Charlie, when did this start?" Carson exclaimed.

"During the test flight at Accra," he replied calmly. "Don't worry about it. Chester and I have developed a half-hour after-start check that resets most of the circuits. Then we put tape over the rest of the lights."

The good news was that the cabin pressure system worked. They headed west.

The flight was a tough initiation into the 748 for Carson. The weather was bad most of the way to Iceland. They had to change altitudes frequently to avoid icing. On the IFR approach into Reykjavik, the flaps would not go down.

This was a big problem. The runway was short and it was reported to be slippery. I quickly told Floyd how to manually extend the flaps using a crank back in the cabin near the trailing edge of the wings. It was turbulent as hell and we were bouncing all over the place. Carson went back, found the handle, rammed it into the slot and started turning. He was turning the crank with one hand and trying to hold on with the other. It wasn't doing any good. I yelled for more.

The flaps never went down. Carson didn't have the handle in far enough. Charlie slowed the airplane down as much as he dared, taking into account the ice they were carrying and the turbulence. He knew the strong wind would give them a reduced touch down speed, which would help, but there was a lot of water on the runway. Charlie touched down early and hard. Initially the tires locked and skidded. He pumped the brakes and varied the engine power to help keep the airplane straight. They stopped just before the end of the runway.

Carson ended up on the floor. He complained to Charlie afterward, that he had five hours as a pilot in an HS 748 and still hadn't seen a landing.

I introduced Floyd to Sven Bjorson at the FBO. He gave us a ride over to the Loftleider Hotel. We washed up and went for dinner. Shortly after we sat down, the head waiter came to our table and said, "Excuse me Captain Vaughn, there are two young ladies in the lobby who have asked to speak with you."

Floyd couldn't believe it. He asked what kind of set-up did I have going for me in Iceland. I told him that I didn't know anything about the girls, so we both went to the lobby to check them out. They were two good looking French girls in their early '20s. They introduced themselves and explained that they were flying a Partenavia from France to North America on a practise run for an air race. They didn't have any charts for Canada, so they had received my name from Sven at the FBO. I dug out my charts from the room and had the hotel make copies for them. We talked to them for awhile in the bar. They were travelling with one of the girl's fathers who, it appeared, was financing the trip. We got the impression that they were nice girls who didn't know much about international flying.

The next morning, the girls took off shortly after Charlie and Carson arrived at the FBO. Charlie worked on the airplane and found that the flap problem was a sticking flap clutch. He fixed it with WD-40 and they were on their way to

Godthab, the capital city of Greenland located part way up on the west coast.

When we were talking to Sondre Strom radar, the controller asked us to try and establish contact with a Partenavia that was more than an hour overdue from Reykjavik to Godthab. It was the French girls. The controller had everyone flying nearby calling them to no avail. When we were close to Godthab, they were two hours overdue with no word. The weather was good, so we surmised that they must have had a mechanical problem. There had been no contact made by any of the overflying airliners.

On the approach to Godthab, the controller told us the girls had been found. They had just contacted Sondre Strom. Their explanation for being overdue was that it was a nice day, so they had turned their radios off and flown the long way around the southern tip Greenland and up the other side to enjoy the coastal scenery!

At Godthab, Carson couldn't believe the short runway clinging to the edge of the Fiord. He asked Charlie if he was sure he could stop on that short strip.

"Sure," he replied, "As long as the flaps work."

They did.

When they taxied out for the final leg to Gander, Carson asked Charlie if he was sure the runway was long enough to take off. It was, but Charlie jokingly told him that it wasn't.

"Floyd had cracked jokes all the way from Shannon. I was just trying to return the humour. I told him that the runway wasn't long enough, but there was a 100-foot drop to sea level off the end, and we would use that to gain flying speed."

"What happens if one engine quits on takeoff?" Floyd asked.

"Same procedure as the double engine failure," I replied.

"What's that?"

"Run to the back of the airplane, open the door and jump out."

"Thanks a lot."

Both engines worked and they made it. Five and a half hours later they arrived at the Eastern Provincial Airlines base in Gander, Newfoundland.

Earlier in the delivery, I had been talking to Henry Steeles, the president of Eastern Provincial Airlines. I informed him that the airplane was not in very good condition. When we met him in Gander, I said that the airplane was okay. "By now, we have fixed nearly everything!"

CHAPTER TWENTY-ONE

1983 - Test Pilot

"Whenever a young pilot asks me how I get the flying jobs that I do, I tell them that they don't come easy. You have to be willing to invest in the training, get all the experience you can, no matter how menial and you have to get around and meet the people in aviation who are making things happen. Of course, it helps to be in the right place at the right time."

Charlie Vaughn

In 1983, Charlie was in the right place at the right time. De Havilland Aircraft in Toronto began flight tests on its prototype Dash 8, a 30-passenger, twin-engined turboprop commuter airliner. At the time, the company was manufacturing the 19-passenger Twin Otter and the short takeoff and landing Dash 7 commuter airliner.

Charlie had a few hours as a copilot in Dash 7s from a ferry flight with Wes McIntosh and Peter Dickens. Mick Saunders, de Havilland's chief of flight operations, asked Charlie to fly copilot on a Dash 7 from Toronto to Egypt. Charlie agreed. When his qualifications were submitted to the insurance company covering the airplane for the delivery, he was rejected because of a lack of experience on type.

Mick Saunders told me the bad news. He said that they may have something else for me instead. He called back and offered me a test pilot position on the prototype Dash 8.

"We don't have insurance on that airplane," Saunders said, "and nobody is type checked on it, so you're qualified."

They had pulled one of their experienced Dash 7 pilots off the Dash 8 flight testing program and sent him to Egypt.

I spent a good part of the next year flying as a copilot on Dash 8 test flights with de Havilland pilots Bob Fowler and Wally Warner. These guys were the experts and I learned a great deal about airplanes that I didn't know. We conducted flutter test flights and antenna patterns. I went down to Marana, Arizona, to fly for hot and high flight tests with Wally.

I was allowed to act as captain on some of the flights out of Downsview. When we were done, I received one of the first Type Endorsements on Dash 8s. This came in real handy. When de Havilland started delivering Dash 8s around the world, I got the call.

It proves how devious a path an aviation career can follow. For a long time I had really wanted to fly for Trans Canada Airlines, but by now, I was glad that I had been rejected.

CHAPTER TWENTY-TWO

May, 1985 - Sri Lanka

*"There will be rebel infiltrators watching. Change out
of your pilot shirts and become departing tourists as
soon as you can."*

Bill Deluce

In early 1985, Austin Airways sold one of its Hawker
Siddeley 748s to the Sri Lankan Air Force. Sri Lanka is a
large island off the southern tip of India. It was formerly the
British colony of Ceylon. Populated by mostly Singhalese, it
received independence in 1948. In 1985, the island nation
was in a civil war between the Hindu Tamil Tigers and the
Singhalese government. The war was heating up with the
rebels receiving some backing from the Indian government.

The Sri Lankan Air Force officials needed a large airplane
to haul fuel to the war zone on the north end of the island.
They connected with Bill Deluce. His family owned Austin
Airways based in Timmins, Ontario. They were selling their
HS 748s and replacing them with de Havilland Dash 8s. Bill
Deluce made a deal with the Sri Lankans on a 748 that
included the installation of aluminum cabin fuel containers
that turned the airplane into a tanker.

Austin chief pilot Jack McCann called Charlie and asked
him if he would do the flight, including making all the enroute
arrangements for the delivery.

I was not interested in starting my own ferry company, but
it was no big deal to arrange a trip like that. I had my own set
of charts that were more up-to-date than any loaned to me on
a contract delivery. I just had to arrange for overflight
clearances and fuel along the way.

I flew to Timmins, met Jack McCann and saw the airplane. The cabin tanks were being installed at Austin's maintenance hangar. I also met Bill Deluce and his younger brother Joe. They were two of the five sons of Stan Deluce, Austin's owner. Bill advised me to plan to fly outside of Indian airspace and to make no contact with them. "India is supporting the rebel cause, so it is basically at war with Sri Lanka," he warned. "You can count on their intelligence knowing when the airplane is coming, so steer clear."

Joe Deluce was to be my copilot. He was a round, easy-going guy in his mid-thirties. He turned out to be a fine pilot and a good man to have on a trip.

Charlie was one of the first pilots to regularly use a Loran navigation receiver in an airplane. Loran was a marine navigation aid that used low frequency transmitters set up in the coastal areas in many parts of the world. The signals were good for long distances.

Charlie bought marine Loran receivers from Harry Mosher before they became available for airplanes. Mosher was a St. Catharines-based radio technician and amateur pilot who serviced navigation equipment for the shipping industry on Canada's Great Lakes. By the time of the Sri Lankan trip, Charlie had a dual chain marine receiver with an airborne software card. It was a bread box-sized unit made by Internav, a Canadian company based in Sydney, Nova Scotia. Charlie was one of the first to try it. At Internav's request, he kept track of signal strengths and reception quality using the unit in different parts of the world.

I didn't have the new Arabian Sea chain of frequencies in my Loran. We were going to need them to avoid Indian airspace. Bill Deluce provided me with a return airline ticket to Nova Scotia. I took my Loran to Internav and waited while they installed the new frequencies. Back in Timmins, the engineers installed the receiver standing on its end between the two pilot seats.

On April 30, Charlie went to Timmins to pick up the airplane and to meet his passengers. The Sri Lankan Air Force had sent two pilots to Canada to fly back with the airplane, a squadron leader named Weerakody and a captain named Anselm.

Joe Deluce said the airplane had been test flown on the cabin tanks and that everything was ready. We planned to depart the next morning. Bill Deluce gave me specific instructions before we left. He said that Joe had a full money belt with him and we were to use it to entertain the two Sri Lankans along the way. "Show them a good time," he said. "Their air force has indicated that they may buy two HS 748s and we have another one to sell. Call me at every stop no matter what time it is here. Sri Lanka has not paid the balance owing on this airplane yet. We are assuming they will, but you will not be arriving in Sri Lanka until they do."

Bill also warned us not to contact India and to get out of Sri Lanka as soon as we make the delivery. "There will be rebel infiltrators watching," he said, "Change out of your pilot shirts and become departing tourists as soon as you can."

We got away mid-day on May 1. The airplane was tankered with wholesale fuel at Timmins so we could have flown non-stop into the night, but we planned an entertainment stop in Gander. I knew a restaurant there that served great lobster so I promised the Sri Lankans a true Canadian feast.

We flew to Gander in 4.4 hours arriving in plenty of time for dinner. We went to the restaurant and I ordered lobster for all of us. The waitress said they didn't have any. Joe gave me a ribbing over that one, but the two air force pilots didn't care. Neither of them had been out of Sri Lanka before. They were just happy to be entertained.

The next morning was cold and the airplane was covered in frost. We had to have it de-iced, a procedure the Sri Lankans had never seen. It was an education for Joe as well. He had never flown far from home and had never paid for a de-icing out of his pocket.

We departed for Shannon $600 lighter. We had to burn off some fuel to be able to climb to 17,000 feet, but once there, we picked up a good tailwind and landed at Shannon, Ireland, 7.3 hours later.

I knew that Shannon would not let us down for entertainment and I was right. We started with drinks at Durty Nellies Pub and then went across the Shannon River for dinner in Bunratty Castle. Bunratty is a Medieval castle turned into a restaurant. The famous Bunratty singers are the waitresses. We were served an Irish version of a Henry VIII dinner with generous quantities of meade, platters of food, daggers for knives and lots of old Irish songs.

A lot of pain was loaded onto the 748 the next morning. The cabin fuel tanks gave us range for further, but we had not received overflight clearances for Egypt, so we planned to stop in Iraklion, Crete. The weather was good and the flying was easy so Joe and I spelled each other off by giving the Sri Lankans a turn in the pilot's seat. We had done no flying with them before the trip so we watched them closely. They didn't have any trouble with straight and level flight with Joe or I setting up the navigation radios. We landed at Iraklion 8.6 hours later.

It is difficult to communicate out of Crete. When Joe and Charlie finally got in touch with Bill Deluce the next day, he told them to stay put. Sri Lanka had not paid for the airplane. He also said that they should keep the two air force pilots in sight so they would not take off with the airplane on their own.

We rented a car and took a three-day, grand tour of Crete. We stopped at every scenic vista, historic sight, nude beach and restaurant on the island. I think this was the only delivery flight on which I gained weight.

On the third day, we received an overflight clearance for Egypt. Bill Deluce allowed us to fly to Luxor, in central Egypt. We would wait there for his okay to proceed on the pretence that we couldn't get an overflight clearance for Saudi Arabia.

The two Sri Lankans loved Luxor. One block from the Nile River takes you back 600 years. The pilots had a great time haggling in the market for ornate brass trays to take home as gifts. We toured the ancient temple in nearby Karnak and the tombs of the Pharaohs in the Valley of Kings.

Weerakody and Anselm enjoyed being treated so well, but after a couple of days in Luxor, the tourist experience was wearing thin. It was their first time away from home and their country was involved in a civil war. They were getting anxious to get back. They were gracious about it, but they must have suspected that we were stalling the trip for more than an overflight clearance.

Joe and I grew to like the two Sri Lankans. We didn't enjoy guarding against them stealing the airplane. We also didn't like the uncertainty of not knowing the next step or when it might occur. We knew it was possible that Bill would tell us that the deal was off, to dump the Sri Lankans and fly back to Canada.

On the third day, we had to move out of our hotel to Thebes across the river. The area was booked solid for the tourist season. This didn't help anyone's frame of mind. Neither did the 40 degree C heat. By the fifth day, the strange food, the crowded streets and the baking temperatures had turned an interesting tourist experience into an irritating waiting game. Bill received payment for the airplane that day. He called Joe and said we could finish the delivery.

As anxious as we all were to get going, we decided to wait until that evening. The performance figures for the HS 748 didn't cover heat near ISA +35. We knew it would be sluggish.

To leave Egypt, the crew needed stamps of approval from the weather office, customs, immigration, the health inspector and airport control. This was not new to Charlie, but the hot weather and the wait affected the way he handled it.

I was tired of everyone asking for a hand-out. Nagi, the health inspector, was a good example. He didn't come right out and ask for twenty bucks. He hummed and hawed over alleged discrepancies in the health certificates. There was nothing wrong with them. He was fishing for a bribe. I told him to stop fooling around and to stamp the flight plan. He was offended, but he didn't give up on his payoff. He said that he would stop by my hotel before we left. He told me what time and I said, "Sure."

I arranged not to be at the hotel when he came. He was waiting for me when we went out to the airport that evening. He gave me a long story about having to raise a family on a servant's wage and how visiting pilots should be "more cooperative". To get rid of him, I told him to take up his complaint with General Ansari. When Ansari had been a colonel in the Egyptian Air Force, I had delivered de Havilland Buffalos with him. He obviously hadn't fallen out of favour yet, since the mention of his name turned Nagi into the humble civil servant.

The four pilots departed in the cool of the evening of May 11 and flew all night to Muscat, the capital of Oman on the eastern tip of the Arabian Peninsula. They were able to get a quick turnaround that included catering for an enroute lunch, something unheard of in the rest of that part of the world. They departed for Sri Lanka in the early morning of May 12. The plan was to fly non-stop to Colombo, the national capital of Sri Lanka, by crossing the Arabian Sea into the Indian Ocean. They were going to use the GPS to remain beyond the 200-mile limit of Indian Airspace, as ordered by Bill Deluce, but India controlled the ocean airspace beyond its international borders.

Muscat Control ended halfway across the ocean. When we were leaving his airspace, the controller told us to contact Bombay Control, which we didn't want to do. We didn't want India to know we were there. The Sri Lankan pilots had explained that if the airplane was forced to land in India, it would result in their execution. Muscat insisted that we had to talk to Bombay if we wanted to proceed. We were flying under the aircraft's Canadian registration, but we hadn't applied for an Indian overflight clearance. We knew they would figure out from our destination, what was going on.

I called Bombay Control and requested a routing well outside of India's international limits, but inside their ocean airspace. The controller was hostile right from the beginning. "You do not have an Indian overflight clearance," he said. "Remain outside of Indian airspace."

I had talked my way through India's bureaucracy before, so I told the controller that we did have an overflight clearance and gave him a fake number. He didn't hesitate to tell us that we didn't have a clearance and that we must remain outside of Indian airspace. They obviously knew all about us. I didn't argue any further. We turned southeast toward the Maldive Islands, 300 nm south of India, a detour that added a couple of hundred miles to our trip. We had plenty of fuel thanks to the cabin tanks, but the Sri Lankan Air Force was expecting us at a certain time.

I called Colombo on our high frequency radio to extend our time of arrival. The call was intercepted by Madras Radio in India. That controller repeated warnings about staying clear of Indian airspace. I could hear Colombo also calling us back on the same frequency but I didn't reply to either of them. I wasn't sure if the Indians could home in on our HF transmissions so I didn't make any more calls.

The detour took us beyond Loran coverage which left us with dead reckoning navigation. The Sri Lankans were asleep in the back. When they woke up and came forward, they saw the Eight Degree Channel Islands. They thought it was the Maldive Islands which would have meant that we were way off course. They both got very excited. It took awhile to calm them down and explain where we were.

The two Sri Lankans remained nervous. As we approached Colombo, the radar showed the Indian coastline off to our left. We made contact with Colombo on the VFR radio 100 miles out so they knew we were coming. The weather was good so I put Weera in the left seat for the landing. It was a good move. He was very proud and was happy to be seen as the captain of the airplane.

As ordered by Bill, Joe and I planned to change out of our pilot shirts and lay low in a hotel until we could get an airline flight out. We didn't count on the Sri Lankan hospitality. The air force had laid on a party for us that evening. They would not entertain any suggestions other than a full military reception. It was an opportunity for the two pilots to return the good time that we had shown them on the flight over. It was quite an emotional send off with tears in the eyes of the two Sri Lankan pilots.

CHAPTER TWENTY-THREE

November, 1985
From Brussels or bust

"I've learned all the systems on the HS 748 by having trouble with them."

Charlie Vaughn

At the end of October, 1985, aircraft broker Floyd Carson asked Charlie to deliver another HS 748, this time from Brussels, Belgium, to Oshawa, Ontario (near Toronto). He promised that the trip would go a lot smoother than their Ghana experience. This 748 was to be one of the launch airplanes for Oshawa-based Intercity Airlines.

The airplane had been used for airways calibration flights in Germany. During that time, its cabin would have been crammed with radio navigation equipment. When I first saw it, the radios had been stripped out of the back, but all of the wiring harnesses had been left. Apparently, the airplane had been sitting for a long time. The cockpit equipment was intact, but it turned out that none of it worked. I discovered that during a test flight out of Brussels. We reracked the radios and then they seemed to work on the ground, but they didn't last long. This 748 had the larger engines which gave it lots of power, but left it short on range.

I departed Brussels for Shannon, Ireland, on November 3 with Bob Reeves, an ex-Calm Air pilot in the right seat, and Floyd as a passenger. As we left the coast we lost our gyro instruments and all our navigation radios except the portable Loran that I had installed in the observation bubble. By the time we got to Shannon, we were down to a standby compass and the Loran.

Shannon was only 3.1 hours from Belgium, but Floyd had had such a good time at Durty Nellies Pub there on the

Ghana trip, that it was now a mandatory overnight stop on any Carson ocean crossing. The next day we flew to Reykjavik. The weather was bad, but the de-icing boots worked. With radar vectors and the Loran, we didn't have any trouble.

It was a different story for a Philippine registered Cessna Citation that landed behind us. He ran out of gas taxiing to the ramp. There were two Filipinos on board, the pilot and his hard driving boss. They had flown from England to Iceland on their way to the United States. They had become lost and were down to fumes when they flew into Iceland radar coverage. The controller vectored them into Reykjavik. When the pilot met the three of us at Sven Bjorson's fixed base operation, he wanted to pay Carson to fly with them the rest of the way. Floyd declined. We never heard of them again, so I hope they made it.

The next leg presented a problem for the HS 748 crew. Their compass systems were so unreliable that Charlie would only plan to land at airports that could give them radar vectors for the approach. Narsarssuak was the best stop on a direct route, but the weather there was reported as zero/zero in fog. It was forecast to improve, but there was no radar vector approach available there. Charlie planned to land at Godthaab with Sondre Strom as the alternate.

Godthaab took us out of our way, but it was the safer route. When we were over Kulusuk, Greenland, the weather reported for Narsarssuak was better. Floyd wanted to go there, but if we did and didn't get in, our fuel to an alternate would have been questionable. I compromised and changed our destination to Sondre Strom where there was radar available. It was south of Narsarssuak, but not as far off course as Godthaab.

We got into Sondre Strom okay. We refuelled and flew to Frobisher Bay, now Iqaluit, on Baffin Island in the Northwest Territories. It was late and we were tired when we checked into the hotel. We had flown three legs from Ireland in one day, but sleep was not to be had. We had picked a Friday night in Frobisher. Every time I managed to dose off, I was awakened by either a fight outside my door or the fire alarm.

The next morning, the three pilots dragged themselves out to the airport and flew to Oshawa with a stop in LaGrande, Quebec, for fuel.

Neither one of us was alert enough to deal with any kind of emergency. Fortunately, the weather was good along the way and we had no further trouble with the airplane.

CHAPTER TWENTY-FOUR

October, 1987 - Hatchet job

"I don't carry hatchets."
Charlie Vaughn

On October 9, 1987, Michael Bannock of World Wide Aircraft Ferry called Charlie. Bannock, son of well-known de Havilland pilot, Russell Bannock, had started a ferry service based in Toronto. Charlie had already done some work for him. This time, Bannock asked Charlie if he could "bury the hatchet" with Glen Code long enough to fly a de Havilland Twin Otter from Scoresbysund, Greenland, to Calgary. The airplane's nose had been damaged during a landing accident. A mobile repair team from Field Aviation had done a temporary fix and installed a cabin fuel system so the airplane could be flown to Calgary. Glen Code had gone to Greenland with a young copilot, but before the airplane was ready to fly, the copilot had received a call from an airline offering him a job starting immediately.

The "hatchet" referred to by Bannock was the HS 748 delivery to Sri Lanka that Charlie had done for Austin Airways. Apparently, Code had considered Austin his own territory and Charlie had invaded it. But now he was stuck in Greenland needing a copilot. He told Bannock that he would bury the hatchet if Charlie would.

I told Michael that I didn't carry any hatchets. The aviation world is too small for grudges. Sooner or later, they catch up to you.

I left for Greenland the next day, but it took me two days to get there. I flew the airlines from Toronto to New York with a stop in Philadelphia. Then I flew on Icelandair to Keflavik, rode a bus to Reykjavik and hitched a ride on a Greenlandair

Dash 7 freighter to Scoresbysund. Fortunately, I was travelling light. Michael had told me that Greenlandair was supplying the survival equipment and that Glen Code had everything else we needed.

Scoresbysund is a small village clinging to the east coast of Greenland, 500 miles north of Iceland. A group of portable buildings had been set up as a base camp for oil exploration in the area.

Glen was true to his word and was friendly. So was I. He showed me the airplane as soon as I arrived. The team from Field had rigged an angle iron repair to the broken nose gear and had set up six 45-gallon fuel drums in the cabin with gravity feed to the airplane belly tanks to give extra range. I strung an antenna from a clamp on the right landing gear leg to the tail skid for my Loran. We planned to leave the next morning.

Charlie didn't know it at the time he was installing his antenna, but without the Loran, the trip across Greenland would have much more difficult. It turned out that the airplane's compass was unreliable and the non-directional beacon on the west coast was out of service. There were no VORs.

There were also no telephones or other methods of communication for checking weather and filing flight plans. Charlie and Code departed the next day, October 12, on a Flight Itinerary. They knew the weather was good at Scoresbysund and they knew that they had enough fuel to fly across Greenland and back, if necessary.

The two pilots used the Loran to navigate the snow-swept ice cap of central Greenland to Godhavn, on the west coast. They refuelled and flew southwest across Davis Strait to Frobisher Bay on southern Baffin Island. They landed in the early winter darkness, cleared customs and stayed overnight.

The next day we planned to fly to Churchill, Manitoba, and then on to Calgary, but a large area of bad weather and strong headwinds lay across the route. It was Glen's idea to dogleg around the bad weather and avoid the worse of the headwinds. We flew a more southerly course to Timmins. It took eight hours to cover the 1,000 nautical miles. We were both tired from the long previous day so we stayed overnight at Glen's place near Timmins.

It took the two pilots another eleven hours of bucking headwinds over the next day and a half to reach Calgary.

After 27 hours of flying together over three and a half days, we were friends again.

CHAPTER TWENTY-FIVE

March, 1988
Italy was supposed to arrange it

"I didn't consider it unusual to be dodging thunderstorms over the ocean while navigating by only time and heading. I used a circular flight computer just like student pilots do. It works."

Charlie Vaughn

Charlie was working outside on the family farm when Robina took a phone call from Italy. "Would Captain Vaughn fly a Partenavia P-68TC from the factory in Naples, Italy, to Brisbane, Australia, as soon as possible?" the caller asked.

"I'll get him to call you back," Robina said.

The caller worked for the Partenavia factory in Italy. He told Charlie that one of their airplanes was scheduled to go on display in the Italian Pavilion of Expo 88 and all of their pilots were busy.

Charlie had never flown a Partenavia. He liked flying different airplanes to new destinations. He said he would do it.

The next day Charlie flew to Rome via Alitalia out of New York City. In his baggage he carried what he had learned were the necessities of ferry flying: an inflatable life raft, survival gear, an emergency locator transmitter, a portable Loran, charts, tool kit and toilet paper.

The toilet paper was for the Arab countries.

It took a full day in Rome to obtain an Italian pilot licence. I needed it to legally fly an Italian-registered civilian airplane. The licence was supposed to be pre-arranged, but I couldn't make the Transport officials understand me. I'd still be there if a young, English-speaking airline pilot from Sardinia hadn't offered to translate. That is one of the unique things about ferry flying. It seems wherever you go, there is always someone willing to help.

The Partenavia P-68TC is a twin-engined high-winged fixed-geared airplane about the size and capacity of a Piper Aztec. Charlie spent three days in Naples working with the Partenavia mechanics while they installed long-range cabin fuel tanks and his Loran. There was no one available to check him out so he studied the pilot manual for the airplane and sat in it while they were getting it ready.

The P-68 he was to fly was a new airplane that had been test flown before the tanks were installed. To save time, Charlie decided to launch on the delivery for his first flight in a Partenavia.

I had a week to make it to Australia. It sounds like plenty of time, but I knew there would be delays through the Middle East. I departed Naples with the airplane weighing 500 pounds over its normal maximum weight. I had 15 hours of fuel on board, so I flew diagonally across the Mediterranean Sea to Luxor in central Egypt.

My first stop became a three-day wait for permission to overfly Saudi Arabia. It was supposed to be pre-arranged by the factory in Italy but it wasn't. I nearly ran out of toilet paper.

Then I flew across the Red Sea and Saudi Arabia to Abu Dhabi, the chief emirate of the United Arab Emirates. I knew it was a treat to stay there overnight, but I had wasted so much time in Luxor, I refuelled and headed straight for Madras, on the far side of India.

This leg of the trip took Charlie across the Arabian Sea and the lower half of India. The distance was over 1,500 nm. He navigated by Loran and VOR, arriving in Madras late at night.

After a short overnight, Charlie headed across the 1,400 nm stretch of the Bay of Bengal to Kuala Lumpur, Malaysia.

I followed dead reckoning most of the way, Charlie said. The beacon on Nicobar Island was shut off and there was no Loran coverage in that area. Thunderstorms forced me to make several timed deviations from my intended track.

Charlie did not consider it unusual to be dodging thunderstorms over the Indian Ocean while navigating by only time and heading.

I used a circular flight computer to keep track of my changing distance and estimated time of arrival just like student pilots do. It works.

Ten hours later, Charlie picked up the Medan VOR on the island of Sumatra. He was 30 miles off course. The next stop was Darwin, on the northern tip of Australia where he had to clear the Partenavia into the country.

The navigation along the Indonesian islands was easier. The mountainous scenery was spectacular. The Australian customs arrangements were supposed to be done. They weren't. I sorted things out and arrived in Brisbane on the east coast of Australia three days before Expo 88 began. There was just time enough for the airplane to be cleaned and transported to the Italian pavilion.

Seventeen days from when he set out for Italy, Charlie was back on the farm tying grapes after a solo flight half way around the world.

CHAPTER TWENTY-SIX

June, 1988 - Rather fly than eat

"I was so tired and hungry that I called Bill by another name. He was so tired that he answered me."
Charlie Vaughn

On June 26, 1988, Charlie flew to Dulles Airport in Washington, DC, on the airlines and took a taxi to Leesburg, Virginia. Michael Bannock had arranged for him to pick up a Piper Seneca III and deliver it to Brussels, Belgium. The twin-engined, piston-powered Seneca can be flown by one pilot, but Charlie asked Bill Salton to go with him. Salton was a young St. Catharines pilot looking for multi-engine flying experience to further his aviation career. Charlie enjoyed helping pilots get a leg up by taking them on some of his trips. Having Salton along gave him someone to talk to on a long transatlantic crossing. It made the flight more interesting.

I had ordered one of the new compact Lorans from Tom Sternig in Toronto, but it didn't arrive before I had to leave for Leesburg. The Seneca was scheduled to have ferry fuel tanks installed in Bangor, Maine, so I asked Bill to wait for the Loran and arranged to meet him in Bangor.

It was the beginning of a typical ferry trip. When I arrived in Leesburg, the airplane was locked and no one on the airport had a key. It took me several phone calls and a good part of the afternoon to get into the airplane.

I finally took off at 18:00. I remember thinking that I was fortunate not to be departing across the ocean on the first leg of the trip. The four-hour flight from Leesburg to Maine gave me a chance to check out the aircraft's radios and systems and to prove its fuel and oil consumption before heading over the water.

My late departure put me into darkness for the last hour of the flight. This would not have been a problem except one of the engines developed a misfire. It was then I realized that flying over the bush in Maine at night with a sick engine is less comforting than flying over the ocean. I continued on the theory that there was no where nearer than Bangor to get it fixed. I was lightly loaded and I knew I could fly on one engine. I made it without having to shut anything down.

The next morning, Aero Fusion in Bangor installed ferry tanks while I traced the misfire to a bad ignition lead. That afternoon, I flew to an FAA office in Concord, New Hampshire, to pick up a permit for the ferry tank installation. This was like putting the horse after the cart but I didn't tell the clerk that I had flown the aircraft for which I was applying for a permit to fly and he didn't ask.

It was after supper when I arrived back in Bangor. When I selected the landing gear down, nothing happened. It stayed up when I recycled the lever. The circuit breaker was still in, so I used the emergency extension, which worked fine.

I spent the next morning with the Aero Fusion mechanics tracing the landing gear problem to faulty wiring for a microswitch, which we fixed. Bill arrived that afternoon with the new Loran.

Rather than wait around in good weather to install the Loran, we departed for Sept Iles, Quebec, that same day. I knew Jacques Blouin, operator of Gulf Helicopters had an avionics technician in Sept Iles who could rig it for us. I called him and arranged to meet at the Sept Iles Airport that evening.

We flew northbound up the border between New Brunswick and Quebec and across the Gaspé Peninsula. Jacques was waiting for us when we cleared customs at Sept Iles. It didn't take him long to rig a temporary mount for the Loran on top of the instrument panel and to clamp the antenna to the rear door frame.

There was nothing to eat at the Sept Iles Airport. I was hungry and tired from a few skipped meals and short nights over the previous two days. Jacques offered to run us into town to eat or spend the night, but the weather was still good and we knew the daylight would last a long time in June. Bill was keen to keep going so we took off for Goose Bay, Labrador, three hours away.

Bill flew that leg while I tried to figure out how to work the Loran. Apollo sold a lot of 604s. They were supposed to be user friendly, but not when you're as tired as I was. I sat with the manual on my lap and could not figure how to extract anything more than distance from it.

Goose Bay turned out to be a poor choice to stop overnight. The two pilots learned that there were no hotels available. They thought of going into town to eat but were told that the restaurants would be closed. There was no food or accommodation at the airport but they were welcome to sleep on the floor of the terminal building, which they tried to do.

I thought we could go into town for breakfast in the morning, but neither of us could sleep. Tired as we were, the floor was too hard and the sky was too bright. After tossing for a couple of hours, we decided to take advantage of the good weather and continue our trip. At one o'clock in the morning it was still light outside. We departed for Reykjavik, Iceland.

The sun was below the horizon but there was enough light for Bill to enjoy a good view of the rugged coastline of Labrador and the vast emptiness of the North Atlantic. We crossed the southern tip of Greenland and flew up the east coast. It never did get dark. The sun rose in the northeast sky and lit up the ice-capped mountains in Greenland.

The Seneca III is a turbocharged, piston-engine aircraft which flies most efficiently between ten and fifteen thousand feet. We didn't have supplementary oxygen on board, so we cruised at 7,000 feet in an effort to stay awake.

It's hard to explain to someone who has never done it, why would you push yourself on a ferry flight when it doesn't seem necessary. Sometimes it is just easier to keep going than to stop, so you press on. I was so tired and hungry on the 8.6 hour flight to Iceland, that I started hallucinating. I tried to stay awake by making idle conversation. I confused Bill with Angus Gordon. He was so tired that he answered me.

"You know, Angus," I said, "They sell the best wool sweaters in the hotel in Reykjavik. You'll have to get one for Marlene (Angus's wife)."

"That's a good idea," Bill replied.

In that state of mind and body, you're mentally and physically numb. Your awareness is near zero. If anything unusual had happened, I would have had trouble noticing it. If I had, I would have been hard pressed to care. Thankfully, the weather was good and the airplane ran fine on autopilot. All we had to worry about was staying awake for the landing.

Sven Bjorson took good care of us when we arrived on his ramp. It was late morning Iceland time. As soon as we checked into the hotel, we headed for the restaurant and ordered breakfast. When a plate full of bacon and eggs was placed in front of Bill, he started to heave. He was so tired and hungry, he couldn't eat. I got him to drink some juice and then put him to bed.

The two pilots stayed in Reykjavik for two days to recover from their self-imposed marathon. On July 2, they departed with full tanks for a non-stop flight to Belgium.

We flew over the North Atlantic at 11,000 and later at 13,000 feet. The airspeed was good and we picked up a great tail wind. It looked like we would make Belgium without any problem until the weather turned bad over the North Sea. The Stormscope showed thunderstorms spread across our path. We encountered airframe icing. Shortly after that, one of the engines started to run rough. We were light on fuel by then, but I knew we couldn't hold altitude on one engine with a load of ice. We looked for the source of the misfire.

Moving the mixture to full rich on the bad engine helped, but it still ran rough. The ferry tanks had been vented with a clear plastic hose. I could see that ice had accumulated in the hose. I took the gas cap off the nearest cabin tank. There was a mighty "whoosh" and a "bang" as air rushed in. The engines had been sucking the tank walls in until the vacuum no longer allowed fuel to flow. Both engines would have quit eventually. When I removed the gas cap, the engines ran fine.

We landed in Belgium eight hours after departing Iceland. The trip taught me a lesson about carrying extra food on ferry flights.

The contract for this trip included the requirement that we remove the ferry tanks from the cabin upon delivery of the airplane in Brussels. This would not have been a problem except the tailwind over the North Atlantic had left us with about 50 gallons of fuel and no one on the airport had defuelling capabilities. By the time we removed the tanks we had fuel in buckets, on the ramp, on us and in the belly of the airplane. We had to remove panels underneath to drain it all out. Bill and I treated ourselves to a full day of baths and meals before heading home on the airlines.

CHAPTER TWENTY-SEVEN

July, 1990 - The Crash

"By 1990, I thought I might make it through my aviation career without an accident."

Charlie Vaughn

On Friday, July 13, 1990, Michael Bannock called Charlie and asked him to meet Dick Hutton in Quito, the capital city of Ecuador to ferry a de Havilland DH-5 Buffalo to Calgary, Alberta. Ecuador is a small, mountainous country on the west coast of South America. The Buffalo belonged to the Ecuadorian Air Force. It had been run off the end of a jungle airstrip in the wild Pestaza region of eastern Ecuador. The airplane sustained damage to its nose gear. Field Aviation West, a Buffalo maintenance specialty shop in Calgary, Alberta, had sent a mobile repair team to the jungle strip to make temporary repairs. Ecuadorian Air Force pilots had flown the aircraft to a maintenance base in Quito where the repair team did more work. The aircraft was ready to be flown to Canada for a rebuild.

Dick Hutton had gone to Quito the week before to check out the aircraft. Charlie flew there on Saturday, July 14, and met him that night.

The next day we went out to the airport with Steve Goncz and Brian Cole from Field Aviation. Dick had already checked the aircraft over, run up the engines and taxied around. He expressed concern that the nose wheel steering was not that of a normal Buffalo, but said it was manageable. Later when I was at the controls, I concurred. Dick said to me that the paperwork was in order and the only thing we needed were the Panama and Mexico overflight clearances.

Dick and I completed a walkaround, paying particular attention to the temporary repair to the nose gear. I was satisfied that the aircraft was fit to ferry. We started the engines and noticed that the right one was slow to light off. We attributed this to the rarefied air at the 9,223-foot elevation at Quito. We checked the avionics as much as we could but were unable to check DME and transponder. The Ecuadorian pilots assured us that they were working. With the help of Brian and Steve, we installed the antenna for my portable Loran receiver. We filed a flight plan for departure on Monday, July 16.

Dick and I agreed that he would fly the leg from Quito to Grand Cayman Island and on to Houston as captain. The next day I would fly in the left seat and act as captain to Billings, Montana, and on to Calgary.

We started engines at 06:20 and began to taxi for takeoff. During the taxi the right electrical fuel pump caution light came on. The number two compass sat frozen, so we returned to the ramp to have these fixed. Dick commented that the nose wheel steering was sloppy.

On the ramp we discovered that the right nose wheel tire was going soft. Brian and Steve changed the tire, the compass and the number two HSI. They had us on the go again by 10:20.

The landing gear was bolted down for the flight. The repair team had jury-rigged two pieces of three-inch iron pipe in a "Y" from the damaged nose gear back to the floor of the cargo compartment to hold it in place. What Hutton and Charlie didn't know was that the nose gear was not the original. It had been badly damaged in the accident. The Ecuadorian Air Force had replaced it with a less-damaged nose gear from another wrecked Buffalo.

The Buffalo nose gear has a cam mechanism that centres the nose wheel when the weight is off the oleo in flight so it will be straight during the landing. Three of the four bolts holding this mechanism to the oleo piston were sheared.

We took off at 10:30 and flew via Panama to Grand Cayman Island. The trip was slow. We restricted our cruise speed to 160 knots with the gear bolted down. Approaching Grand Cayman, we had decided to use 25 degrees of flap for all landings and no reverse thrust to minimize the load on the nose wheel. Dick did a good landing, but we both heard a "crack" sound from behind.

While Dick went in to clear Customs, I supervised the refuelling and visually inspected all parts of the temporary repair. I couldn't see any problems. After a 50 minute turnaround, we departed for Houston's Hobby Airport. We deviated around some thunderstorm buildups on the Texas coast and received radar vectors to Runway 04 at Hobby. We learned at this time that our two DMEs and two transponders were unserviceable. Thank you for nothing, Ecuador.

Houston ATC let us in anyway. Our total flying time for the day was eleven hours. We cleared customs and immigration, parked at Atlantic Aviation and went to a nearby motel. On Tuesday, July 17, the weather was bad with a low overcast and light rain. We refuelled, filed a flight plan and explained our transponder problem to the controllers. We were allowed to depart Houston IFR into the overcast for Billings, Montana. During the flight, the weather cleared and we had no trouble.

At Billings, I did another careful walkaround, paying particular attention to the nosewheel area and the temporary repairs. After a 40 minute turnaround, we departed for Calgary. Taxiing out for departure, I commented to Dick again that the nose wheel steering was sloppy but was really no different than it was at Houston.

On the flight to Calgary, we encountered considerable turbulence. We changed altitudes several times in an attempt to avoid it without success. Calgary Approach Control gave us radar vectors for landing on Runway 28. Dick had copied the ATIS and it indicated that we had a 10 knot crosswind from the right. The other runways were closed.

The pre-landing check was completed using the challenge/response method as was done on all previous landings. I confirmed that the nose wheel position indicator showed straight. The crosswind touch down was normal and without drift. We landed on the right main gear first followed by the left and then the nose gear.

The remaining bolt in the nose gear centring mechanism was bent. The oleo piston was jammed in the cylinder and the nose wheel was turned sideways even though the cockpit indicator showed it was straight. When the nose wheel contacted the runway, the force transmitted back from the crooked nose wheel was too much for the temporary repairs.

The nose gear seemed to touch normally and then began to collapse. There was a loud bang, the gear folded completely, the cockpit floor buckled and the nose pitched down to the runway. The aircraft skidded along on its chin. At this point I used heavy braking to help maintain directional control and bring the aircraft to a stop. Flames immediately shot up through the floor.

The collapse of the nose gear ruptured hydraulic lines in the wheel well. Fluid sprayed from the broken lines pressurized at 3,000 pounds per square inch. Sparks from the nose scraping on the asphalt ignited the spray. The result was instant fire in the cockpit.

Flames and dense black smoke filled the flight compartment before I had stopped the airplane on the runway. Dick yelled, "We're on fire — Get Out!"

He didn't have to yell it twice. I couldn't believe how quickly the cockpit could be filled with smoke and flames. Fire shot up my left side high enough to singe the hair off my arm and to burn the left side of my face as I unfastened my harness. Breathing was difficult. Visibility in the cockpit was zero in smoke. I jumped through the flames into the space between the seats and ran through the smoke to the left side cabin door at the back of the cargo compartment. I turned the handle and shoved. It didn't budge. I didn't feel panic, just determination. I slammed all my weight against it and it opened. Because the airplane was down on its nose, it was at least eight feet to the ground. I didn't hesitate to jump.

I ran from the aircraft fearing that it might explode. I looked back thinking that Dick was following me, but he was not there. I thought he might still be inside. If he was, it would have been too late to save him. By now, the flames were coming out the cockpit windows. Both engines were still running.

I looked around and found Dick on the opposite side of the nose. He had exited through the co-pilot's side window in front of the whirling propeller. I trotted over and joined him.

The airport crash crews arrived and killed the engines by pumping foam into the air intakes. This stopped the hydraulic pumps and the fire was quickly extinguished. The airplane was not burned to the ground, but it was so badly gutted, it never flew again.

The Transportation Safety Board of Canada investigated the accident. The nose wheel landing gear was shipped to the TSBC laboratory where the sheared bolts and jammed piston were discovered. The official accident report stated:

"During one of the first flights of the ferry trip, the steering actuator moved sufficiently to shear the upper cam pins, allowing the nosewheel to move off centre. The crew had no reason to suspect that the nosewheel was not centred before touchdown because they had set the nosewheel steering wheel centring mark to the same position on the lubber line as used during previous landings. When the misaligned nosewheel contacted the runway, the resultant overload forces caused the ferry installation to fail, and the nosewheel collapsed into the nosewheel compartment."

The accident taught me a few things. On all flights, hope for the best but expect the worse. Now I check the emergency exits in every airplane that I deliver to make sure they work.

CHAPTER TWENTY-EIGHT

April, 1991 - Papua, New Guinea

*"How are you going to write this chapter without mak-
ing Angus and I look bad?"*

Charlie Vaughn

℃harlie had a particularly troublesome flight across the
Pacific in a slightly over-used de Havilland Twin Otter. Given
the opportunity to do it over again, Charlie said he would still
have taken the flight, but in hindsight he might have done
things differently.

Charlie doesn't have to worry about looking bad. This
chapter is not about how he and copilot Angus Gordon
survived despite themselves, but how they made the best of
several breakdowns and lived to tell about it.

The Twin Otter in question had been purchased in the
United States by the Mission Aviation Fellowship. The
airplane was in Redlands, California, and was to be delivered
to the MAF Mount Hagen base in central Papua New Guinea.
Larry Nicholson, a Canadian from Kitchener, Ontario, and
MAF's chief mechanic in Papua New Guinea, had inspected
the airplane in California. He worked on it and left it in
Redlands where a shop was to complete the maintenance
necessary for the Pacific crossing.

You have to understand that the MAF does not have a lot
of money. Larry Nicholson had planned a complete overhaul
for the airplane, which he could do a lot cheaper in Papua
New Guinea. I have a lot of respect for the MAF and I believe
Nicholson thought the Twin Otter was safe for delivery. The
problems we had could have occurred with any airplane.

On Saturday, April 6, 1991, I flew from Toronto to San
Francisco, California, on the airlines with Angus Gordon. This

would be my first westbound crossing of the Pacific and I knew it would be tight. I have a lot of respect for Angus. He is an excellent pilot with a good head for technical details. He had never flown a Twin Otter so I loaned him the manuals. Two days later he knew more about the airplane than I did.

We were feeling pretty good about the trip when we arrived in California. Michael Bannock had given us three full days notice; the flight out had been uneventful and here we were riding along in the comfort of a stretched limousine.

The van that had been arranged to take the pair to Redlands had broken down, so the taxi company met them with a limousine.

The two pilots arrived in the middle of the Redlands' Airport Air Faire, the local two-day annual air show. Everyone from town was there except the guy we wanted to meet. They found the airplane parked on a corner of the ramp and located their contact by telephone. John Hood was a California-based MAF mechanic. When Hood arrived, the three used the remaining daylight to install a portable Loran receiver and an HF transmitter.

The HF was a "Bannock Special," probably World War II surplus, probably good for 200 miles. We had to buy a motorcycle battery to run it since the airplane was 24 volt and it was 12. The next morning we planned to fly to Oakland, California, to have the ferry tanks installed. Our departure was delayed until we arranged with the Air Faire organizers to include our takeoff as part of their show.

The two pilots waved to the crowd which had no idea that the ex-commuter aircraft performing the unremarkable take-off in front of them was departing on a two-week flight half way around the world. The two hour and 42 minute leg to Oakland gave the pair a chance to check the aircraft's fuel consumption before launching across the ocean. This was important. They knew the Hawaii leg was going to be tight even with cabin fuel.

In Oakland, they met the "ferry tank king," Vic Kos.

Kos is one of the more interesting characters in the ferry world. He is the only one with a crew who will do a ramp-side ferry tank installation in six hours on Sunday complete with a ferry permit. He gave us a 1,000 U.S. gallon capacity by installing six rectangular tanks in the cabin. Each tank was connected to a common fuel manifold up front via a complicated maze of water pipe, valves and clear plastic garden hose. There were no pumps; the system ran from the manifold into the front and rear aircraft tanks in the cabin floor.

When the tanks were filled that night, the gear legs splayed out and the tires squashed down. Angus calculated that we were up to 17,000 pounds. The airplane's normal gross weight was 12,500 pounds.

The first leg to Hawaii would be the longest of the trip. Ocean crossing regulations required that we land in Honolulu with two hours fuel remaining. I don't know what they would have done if we had landed with less. It's kind of like closing the barn door after the cows are out, but I guess they have had a few people run out of gas and land in the drink.

Using the fuel consumption figures from our flight from Redlands, Angus figured our zero wind range, minus the two hours reserve, would be 1,960 nm. This was dependant on getting 150 knots true airspeed at nine thousand feet. The distance was 2,110 nm.

There was no other way to do it except wait for a tail wind. We were prepared to sit until the wind was behind us but we didn't have to. Angus received a good weather briefing that night from Flight Service. We had our tail wind. It was a go for the next day.

The two pilots departed Oakland on April 9 at 06:15, 16 and 17 local time. The heavily loaded airplane needed a lot of runway. The climb was so slow that they needed to get vectors around the Golden Gate bridge. Their best climb was 400 feet per minute at 105 knots. The stall warning light was flickering much of the time. Gordon noted that the one engine would not quite go to its temperature limit at full power, but the difference wasn't significant.

It would be.

They eventually made it to 6,000 feet and decided to level there until burning off some of the fuel. A high speed power setting gave them a cruise of 148 knots. The lower than planned altitude meant a higher fuel consumption, but the initial tail wind was stronger than forecast. They should make it.

Their first problem was the HF transmitter.

It worked on the ground but not in the air. Regulations required that we contact Oakland Centre on the HF radio before reaching the 200 nm limit of VHF communications or we would be told to turn back. I flew while Angus checked the wiring for the radio. He eventually found that the ground wire was hooked up wrong. We were at the 200-nm limit and the controller was getting antsy when we finally made contact on the HF.

The next problem was the cold. It was April in California, but at 6,000 feet over the ocean the temperature was eight degrees Celsius.

We planned not to use the heater because it increased the fuel consumption. We each wore two pairs of pants and most of the rest of our clothes. The trip was becoming reminiscent of the flight from Honolulu to Oakland with Grant Davidson in the Skyvan. On that crossing the heater didn't work, but we stayed warm because we had to take turns hand pumping most of the fuel.

The Twin Otter was well equipped. It had an autopilot as well as Loran, VOR and ADF receivers. We had also installed a portable global positioning satellite receiver. Navigation wasn't a problem. The biggest unknown was the fuel. We could never be sure of our exact fuel burn or what quantity we could get from the ferry tanks. Angus was busy managing the complicated fuel system. It was not a trip that I could have done alone.

We started out going as fast as we could. As the fuel load lightened, we milked the airplane up to 8,000 feet and throttled back. Having a tail wind right off the bat made the ferry flight a lot easier. We knew we would make it long before reaching the point of no return, even if we had lost the tail wind.

When we reached our initial cruising altitude, Angus turned on all the valves to purge any air from the lines. With the clear hose, he could see that they were all working. We logged the fuel burned from the belly tank gauges and recorded the transfer time to replace it from the cabin tanks. Each ferry tank had its own valve, so we could adjust the centre of gravity with the fuel transfer.

Charlie flew while Angus continually reached back and worked the fuel valves like a one-armed pipe organist. At 8,000 feet the temperature was a numbing four degrees. The constant cold was a distraction, but the fifth time Angus transferred fuel from the cabin tanks, he noticed something was wrong. The rate was too slow. Even counting on the reduced head pressure, it wasn't right. The transfer rate was dropping below their rate of fuel consumption.

It was a serious situation. With a dwindling flow of transfer fuel, the airplane's belly tanks would run dry and the engines would quit well short of Honolulu. The two pilots would have to ditch with plenty of unavailable fuel remaining in the ferry tanks.

Angus crawled back through the cabin and found they were not drawing fuel from the rear tanks at all. The long climbs and reduced cruise power had put the airplane in a nose high attitude to the point where the rear tanks would not drain forward. If the two pilots had not noticed the problem and reacted right away, the resulting aft centre of gravity would have prevented them from flying out of the situation.

Our centre of gravity was still not too far aft. All we had to do to restore the fuel flow from the rear tanks was add power and lower the nose. In comparison, the rest of the leg was uneventful. The number two ADF receiver stopped working and we encountered some rain showers near the end of the flight, but there was never another question of whether we would make it.

Flying through rain showers does not sound significant except that the temperature was still only eight degrees and the right door seal on the old Twin Otter leaked. Angus got rain soaked.

Fourteen hours and fifteen minutes from Oakland, they landed at Honolulu.

That's a long time to be cold, wet and worried about fuel. The next leg was going to be almost as long. We took the next day off to catch up on some sleep, fix some minor snags, and work on the unserviceable ADF.

We felt better about our Twin Otter after talking to another westbound pilot who was ferrying a single-engine, single-seat, turbine agricultural aircraft. The radio installation in his cockpit looked like a grade school science project. It was not an assignment I would want. He departed that night to avoid the daytime cumulus. I assume he made it because we never read about him.

On Wednesday, April 11, Charlie and Angus loaded up at first light. Their destination was Majuro, the capital of the Marshall Islands, 1,973 nm away. Their departure was similar to the one at Oakland. They lifted off with the stall light flickering and turned immediately toward the ocean to avoid obstacles.

The two pilots developed a routine. Most of the time, Charlie flew and worked the radios while Angus kept the log and juggled the fuel load. They were feeling more comfortable about the trip at this point.

One hour and 140 nm into the flight, the right engine rolled back toward idle. Weight wise, they were still three or four hours from being able to hold altitude on one engine and they had no way of dumping fuel. They would have to ditch.

There were no warning lights on. Angus hit the igniters, and the engine came back. But it was only a coincidence. By the time we had caught our breath it rolled back again. I radioed a "Mayday" and turned toward Hawaii while Angus went through the emergency checklist. A United States Navy pilot said he was in the area and was heading our way.

When Angus pulled the circuit breaker on the right engine beta switch, the engine came back for good. Beta switch problems are common on Twin Otters. The faulty switch senses the propeller going toward reverse and drives it toward feather, causing the engine to surge. With the circuit breaker out, we could have continued to our destination minus reverse thrust, but we didn't. I knew we couldn't get anything fixed on the Marshall Islands. There were several Twin Otter operators at Honolulu. I cancelled the emergency but continued toward Hawaii.

We were still about 3,000 pounds over normal maximum gross weight when I lined up for a landing. Angus said that it was the smoothest touchdown he had seen me do.

Through the local fixed base operator, Charlie and Angus met George, Honolulu's self-declared Twin Otter expert.

"He was a roly-poly, friendly mechanic who sounded like he knew what he was doing," Charlie said. He confirmed that the beta switch was faulty and proceeded to change it. I asked him why the beta switch had broken. I knew that John Hood had said that he had changed them on both sides in California. George said that it must have been a faulty switch. "It happens all the time," he said.

The FBO receptionist came out to the airplane and said that the local Federal Aviation Administration inspector was coming over to check on the aircraft that had declared the emergency. This little scenario illustrates one of the many ways that ferry pilots can get snagged if they are not on the ball all the time.

George immediately launched into a series of horror stories about the local FAA grounding airplanes. For emphasis he pointed to a Piper Malibu that looked like it had been parked on the ramp for a long time.

We scooped up the aircraft log books and hot-footed it over to the FAA office hoping to head off the inspector. We didn't want him to see our portable radio installations or the Ace Hardware connecting the cabin tanks together.

They found the FAA official in the terminal building. Charlie explained what had happened and told him that George was working on the airplane. The inspector asked if there was anything he could do to help. "No thank you," was the reply.

George finished the repair that afternoon. They ran the engines up and everything worked fine. They had the fuel topped off and were ready to go early the next morning, just one day behind schedule. The engine problem made the pair a little edgy. It was solid ocean all the way to the Marshall Islands except for the U.S. military base on Johnston Island 600 nm from Hawaii.

The HF worked at the required 100 nm call-in, but after that, we had to use VHF to make our position reports at every five degrees of latitude. These we relayed through airliners and military aircraft. The number two ADF still didn't work but the number one was fine. We had Loran navigation until we passed Johnston Island. There is no Loran in the South Pacific but there were enough GPS satellites available to provide navigation for all but two hours on this leg. We could picked up Majuro on the ADF 400 nm out.

The problem with flying that part of the Pacific at low altitudes is the turbulence and associated cloud buildups. It was a long, rough flight requiring almost constant deviations around rising cumulus. At least the fuel was flowing, the engines were running, and it was warm.

By the time the Twin Otter was approaching Majuro, the cumulus had become solid, dark and rainy. It was raining so hard, I could only see straight down. When it was time for a descent, I couldn't raise the Majuro controller for an approach clearance. I knew our radio was working because I could hear an Air Marshall Island pilot in a Hawker Siddeley 748 calling him with the same results. He was behind us and we were holding him up. We both tried Majuro several times. The 748 pilot knew what to do. He just cleared us for a descent on his own.

When Charlie and Angus were on final approach to Majuro Airport, they had been in the air nearly 14 hours, water was pouring into the cockpit through several leaks, and they still couldn't see the runway. Then the right engine began to surge and tried to go into feather. Angus pulled the beta circuit breaker immediately.

The engine returned to normal power. Charlie spotted the runway out his side window.

It was beside us but we had already crossed the threshold. The runway was flooded with rain water and with the beta disabled, I knew we couldn't use reverse thrust to stop. I yelled to Angus, "Do you think I can make it from here?" He still couldn't see the runway, so he said that he didn't know. I went for it.

Charlie got the airplane down and stopped in time. They taxied in slowly through the curtain of rain and shut down on the ramp.

It was hot and humid. We were tired and very wet. We knew that we were now stranded on the Marshall Islands with another broken beta switch. It was very discouraging.

The Majora Airport ramp was built as a catch basin for rain water. The run off fills freshwater cisterns. Three bare-foot native Marshall Islanders waded across the basin/ramp toward the airplane in the pouring rain.

The situation put us both in a bad mood, but sometimes you have to grin and bare it. I climbed out of the pilot's seat and stood under the wing in the boiling mist created by the rain bouncing off the tarmac. The first guy said he was a customs officer and was collecting $43.03. It had to be cash, U.S. dollars. The second native said he was from immigration and, not to be outdone, he wanted $60 U.S. The third guy was the quarantine officer and he asked for $80. None of them wore uniforms. They didn't look in the airplane and they didn't ask to see any documents. I paid them from a roll of wet bills, but made each one give him a receipt, which they did.

It was the late side of a long day. The wet and weary travellers gathered up their gear and took a cab to the nearest motel.

The Marshall Islands are a semi-independent part of the United States Trust Territory of the South Pacific. They are the first group of islands across the International Dateline. Charlie and Angus had landed on the Majuro Atoll which is two islands linked together forming a crescent 30 miles long and slightly wider than the airport's runway. Majuro is also the capital city of the Marshall Islands, population 8,000. It had two hotels. Charlie and Angus stayed at the 12-unit Royal Garden Hotel.

After a good night's sleep I felt a lot better. In the morning I looked out of the room to see the sun shining and the pigs grazing in the Royal Garden's garden.

We had breakfast in the hotel's six-table restaurant. It wasn't very clean. We ordered the fish and rice on the theory that the fish might be fresh and rice lasts forever. It wasn't too bad.

After breakfast, we hailed a taxi from the hotel to the airport. There is a single road running the length of the island. If you need a ride, you just stand by the road and the next car along becomes a cab.

It was Sunday, April 14. The fact that it was a Sunday didn't affect our chances of getting the airplane fixed. We weren't likely to find a Twin Otter expert at Majuro on any day of the week. The one hangar at the airport belonged to Air Marshall Islands. An American mechanic named Greg Grimes was working there. He loaned us a ladder and a few tools.

Angus and I took the cowlings off the right engine and went straight to the beta switch. It was soon obvious why it had failed. The parts around the switch were loose and worn out. The sight gave me bad thoughts about George, the mechanic back in Hawaii. I could see that we could tighten up the switch carrier block and that the carrier ring would probably last a few more hours, but we still needed a new beta switch.

Charlie called Cathy Henderson back at the Panorama fixed base operator in Hawaii. She located a switch and promised to send it out right away. That helped their spirits. They spent the rest of the day securing the loose carrier block with lock wire and readying the airplane for the next leg.

One of the three-times-a-week flights from Honolulu arrived the next afternoon. The part was on the flight. After paying the smiling customs officer more U.S. cash, Charlie and Angus installed the new beta switch and ran the engine. It worked fine. They would check the weather and depart the next day for their final destination, Port Moresby, the capital of Papua New Guinea.

The nearest weather office was Honolulu, nearly 2,000 nm away. Angus found it strange to be flight planning with someone who was working on a different day, but the briefer had satellite shots that would show significant weather in the South Pacific. He said there wasn't any. Angus filed a flight plan for early the next morning.

On Tuesday, April 16, Charlie and Angus loaded their gear on board and taxied out for a first-light takeoff. They were still only three days behind schedule. Charlie ran the turbines up and released the brakes. The right engine wouldn't go to full power. He aborted the takeoff part way down the runway and returned the overloaded airplane to the ramp.

"It wasn't a beta switch problem," Charlie said. We went to the Air Marshall Island hangar to borrow the ladder and tools again. The same mechanic, Greg Grimes, was there. He came out to give us a hand. Greg didn't know Twin Otters, but he and I both figured it must be the fuel controller. I called Honolulu and talked to a Twin Otter mechanic who was reluctant to make a long-distance diagnosis. We went back to the hotel to think about it over lunch.

While we were eating our fish and rice, the hotel had a phone call for us. It was Larry Nicholson, MAF's head mechanic at Mount Hagen in Papua New Guinea. He was telephone tracking along our route to find out why we were overdue. He knew there were only two hotels in Majuro and that the Royal Garden was closest to the airport. I told him our problem and he detailed a troubleshooting sequence that was basically ground run the engine with the power turbine governor capped off to determine if it was a failed fuel controller or the power turbine governor.

Larry was right; it was the power turbine governor which was falsely detecting turbine overspeed and limiting the fuel. I called him back. He said we could fly the airplane with the governor capped off or wait for a new one. He didn't push me but it was obvious from his voice that he was anxious to get the airplane. To fly with the governor capped meant going without overspeed protection over ten hours of the Pacific Ocean. I said we'd wait.

Hawaii didn't have the part. Charlie called Michael Bannock in Toronto who sourced a governor in Canada.

Wednesday the stranded pair took a cab and toured both islands.

The people on Majuro appeared to be poor. Their houses were tin shacks. They didn't have much, but Angus was impressed with their perfect weather and easy pace. He asked the cab driver what a typical house would cost. "Three pickup trucks," was the answer. Since that trip, I think Angus has been saving pickup trucks. When the North American hectic lifestyle finally gets to him, I could imagine him going back to stay.

There was an odd collection of people staying in the hotel. One day we had lunch with an Israeli who was on a contract to teach the Marshall Islanders how to raise chickens. Apparently we weren't the only ones tired of fish and rice. Another day we ate with two men who were running the Chinese Embassy out of the hotel.

On Thursday we bought a few extra tools at the general store so we wouldn't have to borrow Greg's all the time. Angus spotted a sale on raisin bran cereal and vacuum-packed milk. I tried to tell him that hardware stores in Majora are not the best places for milk and cereal specials. The thought of more fish and rice forced him into it. Back at the hotel he discovered the milk was marked "best before April 1989". When he opened the cereal, some of the raisins moved on their own.

With Greg's help, working on his own time, the two removed the old power turbine governor. They were hoping the new one would arrive the following day. It didn't, but they found out it would come the next day, Saturday, April 20. That was the day they had originally planned to be back home. Angus called his wife in St. Catharines and asked her to cancel the aerobatic lessons he was to give that weekend.

Saturday, the governor arrived. Charlie paid the smiling customs officer. They installed the new part and ran the engine. It worked. They would leave the next day.

Larry Nicholson called to see how we were doing. I brought him up-to-date. He said that he would arrange customs at his base in Mount Hagen if we would fly the airplane directly there instead of to the main airport in Port Moresby as planned. That added a couple of hours to our final leg, but saved him at least a day. I agreed. Then he told me that Mount Hagen sat in a valley and at that time of the year it fogged in every day about four o'clock.

It was a 12 and a half hour flight with no wind. With a dawn departure at six am and the time zones, it left us with little window for error. It wasn't a good situation, but I said that we would try.

The two were airborne at 6:02 the next morning. It was

Sunday, April 21. They had been on Majuro a week.

The flight started badly. We got airborne alright, but the HF didn't work, so we couldn't open our flight plan with Honolulu. If we had had to ditch without talking to anyone, our only hope for a search was Larry Nicholson calling Rosie at the hotel to see if we had left.

We had to deviate around showers and buildups right from the start. This added to our flying time, but when we reached an initial cruising altitude of 4,000 feet, the GPS indicated we were getting a healthy tailwind. Our ground speed stayed up for most of the flight which enabled us to use high power settings in the hope of beating the bad weather into Mount Hagen.

The pair were 200 miles from Kavieng, a city on the first crescent of islands in the Bismark Archipelago that guards the approach to the island of New Guinea, and eight hours into the flight before they heard another airplane on the radio. The Australian was able to relay a message to open their flight plan.

There is little traffic on the frequencies in the South Pacific. The first controller that we talked to was Madang Tower on the eastern shore of Papua New Guinea. He was happy to hear from someone. He gave us the current altimeter setting in millibars. Angus couldn't find a conversion chart for inches. I suggested to ask him to convert it for us. He did. This was followed by a very long silence. He was about to ask again when the controller called back sounding proud of his calculation. "67.5 inches," he said. The scale only goes to 34.

When they reached the eastern edge of Papua, New Guinea, they climbed to 15,000 feet to clear the mountains and to top as many cloud buildups as possible. The topography of New Guinea is mostly vertical. They had to cross the Bismark Mountains, including Mount Wilhelm, the tallest at 14,793 feet, to reach Mount Hagen.

"Approaching the destination, the undercast was solid and I was beginning to worry," Charlie said. But up ahead I could see a hole. Through it appeared the airport at Mount Hagen, sitting in a valley. We spiralled down and landed.

The flight had taken 11 hours and 38 minutes. Forty minutes after landing, the valley filled with cloud and fog. The ceiling and visibility dropped to zero. "Just like clockwork," Larry said.

They had flown the Twin Otter a third of the way around the world with three stops. Their total time had been 42.7 hours for the three legs.

Once again they were tired and sore from the long flight and glad to be on the ground. A smiling native customs agent greeted them when they shut down and asked for a clearance fee in cash, American dollars. Charlie paid.

Larry took us to his house that evening. It was in a fenced compound of MAF buildings where he lived with his wife and two young children. Over dinner he explained that Papua New Guinea is one of the most primitive parts of the world. The steep mountains and heavy jungle conspire to keep it that way. He said that the natives were so isolated that several hundred different dialects were spoken on the island. "Communication is difficult," he said, "and travel without airplanes is impossible."

He also mentioned that Mount Hagen had bandits called "rascals" that roamed the town carrying home made shotguns. He and his family had been held up a couple of weeks earlier but no one was harmed. He asked us if we wanted to stay in a house in the compound or at the hotel.

We both answered at once, "We'll stay here."

We talked for a little while about the MAF work in the area. I asked Larry if he honestly thought he was making a difference. "You'll see tomorrow," he answered.

That night I counted three gunshots before falling asleep.

The next morning Larry's wife asked if the earth tremors had kept me awake. I hadn't felt a thing.

After breakfast, Larry took us back out to the airport. His

crew of native mechanics were already working on the airplane. Larry introduced Angus and I using a form of Pigeon English that had enough recognizable words for us to understand. They gave us a round of applause. Larry gathered everyone around the airplane and said a prayer of thanks for the safe deliverance of the pilots and the Twin Otter. Then they immediately started taking the airplane apart for a field overhaul.

Larry suggested that Angus and I ride on a charter flight to a gold mine outpost in their other Twin Otter just to see the operation first hand. Our airline flight to Port Moresby didn't leave until the next day so we agreed.

The pilot was Australian. The destination was a 1,500-foot-long jungle strip cut out of the side of a mountain on a 10 per cent grade at the 7,000-foot level. On the way, the pilot pointed out some of the local landmarks including a wrecked airplane, one of the casualties of operating in the mountainous jungle.

We landed uphill and rolled to the end where there was a little flat spot just big enough to turn around. The pilot set the brakes, shut down the left side engine and hopped out. With the right engine still running, he calmly stood on the dirt apron and sold tickets to the line of outgoing passengers. We were only on the ground for a few minutes. The passengers slung their own bags and we left, taking off downhill. It was a nice piece of flying.

The next day Charlie and Angus said goodbye to their hosts and flew out to the Papua New Guinea capital of Port Moresby on a Tal Air de Havilland Dash 8. There, they were to board an Air New Guinea flight to Sydney, Australia, but their casual customs clearances caught up to them.

Our passports had not been stamped since Hawaii and we had no Australian visa. As far as the Air New Guinea ticket agent was concerned, we were illegally in the country and there was no way he would be responsible for sending us to Australia, only to have the Australians send us back, at his expense.

We had an hour and a half before the flight departed. We grabbed a cab and went to the Australian High Commission office downtown. There was a big sign outside the building that said visas must be applied for 48 hours in advance.

We asked the cabbie to wait. The Aussies were great. They accepted our story and issued visas on the spot using photocopies of our passports for photo identification. The cab got us back to the airport in time, but the outbound customs agent stopped us because we didn't have a visa for Papua New Guinea. These are not required for air crew, but it took a few minutes to convince him that we were aircrew because we didn't have an airplane. We were the last ones on the flight before they closed the door.

The rushing around and fast talking didn't do them much good. They were hoping to catch a flight from Sydney to Toronto the next day, but their tickets were valid for the day after. The Qantas agents readily agreed to exchange them, but when they tried to coordinate with Canadian Airlines, the carrier from Hawaii to Vancouver, the Canadians wouldn't allow it. The pair spent an extra day in Sydney.

It was a one-stop, 27-hour marathon flight home. Of course we were flying "Bannock Class" in the back. The two airliners were full and the stop in Hawaii was only two hours. I think the flight outbound in the Twin Otter was more comfortable.

CHAPTER TWENTY-NINE

April, 1993 - Thailand

"When delivering airplanes around the world, you soon know where you can buy the cheapest fuel, get the best service, and where you can bull your way through the bureaucracy and where you can't. This trip had the best and the worst of all of that."

Charlie Vaughn

At the end of March, 1993, Michael Bannock of World Wide Aircraft Ferry called Charlie. He had a de Havilland Dash 8-300 delivery from Atlanta, Georgia, to Bangkok, Thailand. Mick Saunders would be the other pilot. Saunders had been the chief of flight operations at de Havilland. He was now retired and free lancing.

On April 3, 1995, Saunders and Charlie flew on the airlines together to Atlanta, Georgia, where they were met by Dave Horniak, an engineer for the American leasing company that owned the airplane. Horniak drove them from the Atlanta Airport to Falcon Field where the Dash 8 was parked. There they met Somkiat Chubang, a maintenance engineer for Bangkok Airways. Chubang was in Atlanta doing an acceptance check on the airplane and would ride home to Thailand on the Dash 8 with the two pilots.

We departed for Bangor, Maine, that same afternoon. It was good to have a shake down flight over land and in good weather. It was a bonus to have an engineer on board in case something went wrong. The airplane was not new and had obviously been sitting outside for awhile.

The next day Chubang helped the two pilots install an antenna for a portable GPS receiver. Then they went shopping for groceries while waiting for the export paper work on the airplane.

Chubang was puzzled. He had never flown on an delivery flight before. His only international experience was the airline flights to Atlanta. He politely asked if we thought there would be no food along the way. We told him that there was but you could never be sure what it was or when you might get to eat it. He bought groceries too.

That afternoon they flew 2.7 hours to Gander, Newfoundland.

The Dash 8-300 has a range of 1,200 nautical miles on full fuel, normally enough for a international delivery without extra ferry tanks, especially when flying eastbound with prevailing westerly winds. World Wide Aircraft Ferrying arranged for fuel on a contract price at the appropriate stops along the route.

The next day we got up early and flight planned to Reykjavik, Iceland. We didn't make it. There were headwinds all the way. It took us four hours just to get to Narsarssuak on the southeast coast of Greenland. We landed there and took on just enough fuel for Iceland. Greenland gas is twice the price as in North America.

We flew another 3.3 hours to Reykjavik. We did a quick turnaround there and departed on a flight plan for Rotterdam, the Netherlands. The east wind continued on our nose. After 3.6 hours, we ran low on gas, groceries, daylight and good weather. We gave up trying to make Rotterdam and landed at Newcastle, England, for the night.

So far Somkiat, the Thai engineer, had not said much to us. He was pleasant but quiet. On the ground, he was helpful supervising the refuellings and doing walkaround inspections. When he did talk about the airplane, he sounded like he knew what he was saying, but in flight, he sat back in the cabin by himself.

At Newcastle, we loaded minimum fuel to fly IFR in the rain to Rotterdam. It was a pain to short hop it in the bad weather, but the difference in the fuel price made it necessary.

After a quick turnaround in the Netherlands, we departed for the island of Corfu. On the climbout to 25,000 feet, the left engine suddenly rolled back to idle on its own. No matter what we did, it would not respond to the throttle commands. Somkiat came forward to the cockpit right away. He looked around and calmly said, "I know what that is. It's rain on the cannon plug to the engine control unit. Go back to Rotterdam and I will fix it on the ground."

He spoke with such conviction, that Mick and I didn't question him. We got a priority clearance to return to Rotterdam. During the descent, we got back some limited throttle response on the left engine and landed without incident.

Somkiat borrowed a ladder and took the cowlings off the left engine. He disconnected the cannon plug at the engine control unit. We ran up the engine with the cowlings removed and it worked fine. He cleaned and siliconed the connection and we were back in business. We refiled for the Greek island of Corfu while Somkiat put the cowlings back on. We were back in the air in just over an hour.

Our destination was Kerkira on the west side of Corfu, but we picked up a good tail wind along the way. We extended our flight to Iraklion, in Crete. Iraklion wasn't one of our contract fuel stops but we knew the prices were reasonable there. Besides, Mick and I considered it one of our favourite stops in that part of the world. None of Bannock's planned stops had worked for us to this point, so it seemed appropriate to keep the string going. We stayed overnight in Iraklion, treated Somkiat to a great Greek meal and loaded up on groceries again.

Our next stop was Luxor, Egypt. Luxor was not a favourite stop, but there are not many choices in that part of the world. Mick flew the left seat on that leg and I worked the radios. Getting a quick, low-cost turnaround at Luxor is always a game. The odds are stacked in favour of the Egyptians, but I had played the game before.

When we were taxiing in, the ground controller said that Egypt Air would act as our handlers. "Negative," I replied, "We do not require handling."

We could see the "handler" waving us to a parking spot on the ramp. For that service he would want $300 to $900 U.S., and you don't leave until you pay. I told Mick to park on the other side of the ramp.

As soon as the airplane was stopped, I opened the airstair door and jumped out. The handler came running over carrying his chocks. I waved him off. "We do not want handling," I yelled.

"Oh yes, handling necessary," he said, chocking our wheels. Then he tried to collect. We ignored him.

"I get the police," he said. We continued to ignore him. He went away and came back with a policeman.

The policeman stood on the ramp and listened while the Egypt Air rep gave me what I think was a tongue lashing in Arabic. It sounded like he was calling me every name in the book and he probably was. I told the policeman that I didn't want handling, didn't need handling, hadn't asked for handling and would appreciate it if he would get this handler off my back. Without any further discussion, he said something to the Egyptian in Arabic which sent him away. Then the policeman said that he would be glad to take us through the necessary airport administration. I agreed.

We went through customs, immigration, and airport control. At each stop I placed an American $20 bill on the paperwork. This is customary in Egypt and a lot cheaper than working with a handler. I did the same thing at the weather office and the flight planning office. When we were going back downstairs in the elevator, the policeman said, "Now you can pay me. I offered him $20. He said it wasn't enough. I asked him how much.

"Fifty dollars," he said. I gave him $25. He took it.

We were airborne in one hour and 20 minutes. I was proud of that. It was the shortest and cheapest stop that I had ever experienced in Luxor.

The next stop for the Dash 8 crew was Abu Dhabi. This was another favourite for Charlie and Saunders. A handler named Mahmood worked all Bannock flights through that area on a standing agreement. He was efficient and cheap. Charlie knew him well.

Up to that point we hadn't had much sleep, so we stayed over in Abu Dhabi for an extra day and caught up on rest, meals and groceries. We also took Somkiat on a little local sightseeing tour. "Enjoy this," we warned Somkiat, "India is next."

Our next leg was to Bombay, India. The weather was fine and the airplane ran well. We arrived in the middle of a stifling hot afternoon. In India, you must have a handler or the bureaucrats ignore you. World Wide Aircraft Ferrying had arranged for our handling through British Airways. There was no handler for us when we landed and no one knew who it should be or where he was.

We went through the maze of bureaucracy as best we could on our own. It took a frustrating four hours. If we didn't have the right signatures on the right paperwork in the right order, we had to backtrack through the system until we did.

The biggest mistake we made was to arrange for a lavatory pumpout. If we hadn't been there to yell, the driver would have run the honey wagon right into the side of the airplane. He had a "helper," but he wasn't looking at what the driver was doing. Then the helper opened the dump valve on the lav before hooking up the hose. The sewage spewed onto the ramp. Then the guy wanted to use a fire hose to flush out the lav. I could see the whole airplane being flooded. I managed to stop him and to get the driver to move the truck out of the way.

Our next stop was Calcutta on the other side of India. The bureaucracy there was worse. We arrived at night. The ground controller told us to follow the "Follow Me" truck, which we did. We shutdown where the truck driver indicated. An official from the airport authority came out and said we couldn't park there. The ramp was large and empty. We tried to argue with the guy but that never works in India. Our pre-arranged handler was nowhere in sight.

We moved the airplane and went into passport control without a handler. The immigration official took our passports away and said we could have them back when we were leaving the country. It is not a good idea to be in a country like India without a passport. We tried to argue, but it didn't work.

By the time we got to the hotel, it was after midnight local time. We went to bed tired and hungry. The hotel was hot and noisy. At dawn, we gave up trying to sleep and went back out to the airport. Three hours later, we were airborne. We had no problem on the last leg to Bangkok.

I knew that the Thai officials were good at wrapping visitors in red tape and protocol, but not when you are arriving with an airplane for Bangkok Airways. The airline officials whisked us through the airport officialdom in minutes.

We enjoyed two nights in Bangkok before hopping the airlines home. We flew via Hong Kong and Vancouver, completing the trip by flying around the world.

It hadn't been our best delivery. Mick and I were happy to see the last of that airplane.

CHAPTER THIRTY

September, 1993
Owen Mcdougall

*The copilot's name in this chapter has been changed
for reasons that will become obvious.*

World Wide Aircraft Ferrying called with another de Havilland Dash 8 delivery for Dave Horniak. "Pick up the airplane from Bangkok and fly it to Atlanta, Georgia," Michael Bannock said. "It's a Dash 8-100. Bangkok Airways is returning it in exchange for the 300 you and Mick delivered in the spring."

"Who's the other pilot?" I asked.

"Owen Mcdougall."

"I don't think I know him."

"He's an ex-Transport Canada air carrier inspector checked out in Dash 8s. He'll meet you at the Canadian Airlines counter at Toronto on Wednesday morning. Dave will be in Bangkok to make sure you get under way."

"Okay."

When you spend the best part of two days on an airliner with someone, you get to know them. My first impression of Owen Mcdougall was that he talked too much and knew too little. I could tell right away that he did not have much international flying experience but he was pleasant enough, in a condescending way.

Owen and I met Dave Horniak in the hotel restaurant in Bangkok for breakfast. Dave explained that the Dash 8 was Thai registered and that we had to obtain Thailand pilot licences before we could depart. He added that the airplane did not have a current Certificate of Airworthiness. He also admitted that it had been parked for awhile and that Bangkok

Airways had cannibalized it for parts. It needed work before it could fly, but his maintenance engineer, Larry Wilson was there working with the airline mechanics to get it ready.

This was not the sort of news that a ferry pilot wants to hear, but you learn to expect it.

Horniak took the two pilots to the Bangkok Airways office in the city. The airline officials were going to help them through the paperwork for the pilot licences. The exceptional cooperation demonstrated to Mick Saunders and Charlie when they had delivered an airplane to Bangkok Airways in the spring was gone. Apparently, removing an airplane from Thailand was a different story. They were hit with the full might of the Thai bureaucratic maze.

First they were told that they could not go to the Department of Aviation for licences by themselves. They would have to be escorted by someone from Bangkok Airways and no one was available until Monday. (This was Friday.) Then they were told that they would have to show copies of their overflight clearances for the neighbouring countries before they would be allowed to depart. (The clearances had been pre-arranged by Skyplan International, a company that specializes in such things. Charlie had the clearance numbers but did not have hard copies of the clearances themselves.) Finally, they said that Charlie was too old. In Thailand, pilots over 60 were not allowed to fly commercial aircraft.

Dave was a little embarrassed by all the stonewalling. He argued but the best he could get was agreement that I could act as a copilot on the ferry flight as long as Owen was the captain.

The arrangement transformed Owen. The suggestion that he would be the captain on the airplane went to his head. He assumed royal command and immediately tried to top the Bangkok Airways officials for being a pain in the ass. He declared that he would have to inspect the airplane personally before they went any further.

The Thais took his sudden superior attitude as an insult to the work they were doing on the Dash 8. They told Owen that he couldn't see the airplane until they were finished with it. He countered by saying that he wouldn't test fly it until he had inspected and ground run it completely. That was fine with them. They didn't care if this ignorant Canadian ever took the airplane anywhere.

We had nothing to do but go back to the hotel. On the way, Owen outlined how we would have to test the airplane extensively including flying it to 25,000 feet to check the pressurization system.

I told him that if we got to fly the airplane at all, a test hop around the airport circuit might be a good idea, but our best test flight would be to get the airplane out of Thailand and take it to Calcutta. He ignored what I said and continued to talk about testing the airplane.

That night Dave Horniak called Michael Bannock in Toronto to update him on the lack of progress. He told him the problem that Mcdougall had become. Bannock called Mcdougall in his hotel room and said that his plans for testing the airplane would mean that they would never get it out of Thailand. "Charlie is in charge even if you are the designated captain," Bannock said, "You do what he says."

Then Bannock called Charlie and told him that he had spoken to Mcdougall. "If you have any more trouble, dump him."

"I would," Charlie said, "but it will delay our departure more."

"Dump him anyway," Bannock replied.

I talked to Owen over breakfast and mentioned that I had been talking to Bannock. "I'm in charge," I said as nicely as I could, "but I don't see why we can't get along."

He started talking about the importance of checking the airplane over. "Look, I'm running this operation," I said, this time as bluntly as I could, "We'll do as I see fit and don't you forget it!"

Blunt seemed to work. Owen was more cooperative, but he did find ways to irritate me. He carried on about flight planning details which were meaningless if we couldn't get the airplane released by the Thais.

We were told that Bangkok Airways may be doing run ups on the airplane by the end of the day. They didn't.

September 19, 1993

Progress. We were allowed to do engine run-ups with Somkiat Chubang, the Bangkok Airways maintenance engineer who had accompanied Mick Saunders and I on the previous Dash 8 trip. Owen was good. He didn't say much. We found a couple of minor snags that Somkiat said he would take care of.

September 20, 1993

It looked like we might go. The airplane was ready. The Thai officials said they needed to see our overflight clearance for neighbouring Myanmar (formerly Burma) before they would release us. We didn't have it. After much discussion, they allowed us to do one circuit.

Owen and I sat parked on the hot tarmac with the engines running for a long time before finally getting clearance to taxi for takeoff. There was quite a bit of air traffic using the airport when they released us. It was one busy circuit, but we did get to try everything and it all worked. Owen flew from the left seat and I handled the communications from the right.

That afternoon, our clearance over Myanmar came in. We prepared to depart. Then the Bangkok Airways officials said we needed to show the overflight clearances for the entire route. This was news to us, but they wouldn't have it any other way. I called Skyplan. They said they would fax the whole package to us. The request was new to them too.

September 21, 1993

Charlie and Mcdougall waited all day for a departure clearance which never came. Officially they were told that it was Thailand Customs that was withholding their release. Later on, Charlie found out that Owen had mistakenly filed their flight plan before getting a departure clearance from customs. This was another snub to the Thai bureaucracy that was guaranteed to get them nowhere.

Every day we thought we might be leaving. Every day we checked out of the hotel, went to the airport with our bags and then waited in the Bangkok Airways office. It was a hot, tiring and frustrating experience. We hated to go anywhere in case some news about our departure clearance came through while we were gone.

At the end of the day, we would cart our gear back to the hotel and check in again.

September 22, 1993

The Bangkok Airways officials told the two pilots to expect their departure clearance that day. It never came.

Dave Horniak had to leave. He had worked hard during the last week trying to get us on our way and he felt badly about abandoning us.

September 23, 1993

The airline officials again told us to expect a clearance shortly. We waited around all day. When we asked what the problem was, they said they didn't know. We could only guess that the Department of Aviation was mad for whatever reason and they were trying to teach us a lesson.

At 17:00 we received a departure clearance. We left for Calcutta, India, right away. I put Owen in the left seat. I decided I could handle him better when he was just flying the airplane and nothing else. I worked the radios and monitored what he was doing.

It turned out that he was a good hands and feet pilot but he was irritating. Some people are just naturally like that. They do little things that bug you. If you make a list, it looks trivial, but it bugs you all the same. Owen was constantly fiddling with things in the cockpit that were better left alone. While doing this he would let the autopilot chase after the VOR fluctuations when we were close to the station. I would have liked to dump him, but I didn't want to wait in India for another copilot.

The weather was good to Calcutta. On the ground, we connected with a handler and got a two-hour turnaround, a record for India.

The trip across India to Bombay wasn't as easy. We encountered heavy rain showers halfway across the country. It was dark and getting late. Most airports in India close at night. The Dash 8 carried enough fuel to get us to Bombay with a hold before landing or a diversion direct to the nearest alternate which was Ahmadabad, but not both.

In the bad weather, the static electricity built up and created St. Elmo's fire around the windshield. Owen had never seen it before. He decided that we had been hit by lightning. "What should we do Charlie?" he asked. I could tell by his voice that he was quite agitated.

I tried to explain to him that the blue flame was harmless, but he didn't believed me.

"So what are we going to do, Charlie?"

"Well, let's fly to Bombay," I finally said, "It's the nearest airport."

"Okay, Charlie."

The static charge produced a whine in the communications radios when we were not transmitting. It was something I had never encountered before. The radios worked okay, but the extra noise was annoying.

The pilots in India were not used to flying in bad weather. I could hear the ones ahead of us calling for clearances to their alternates. We continued. On the handoff to Bombay Approach, I couldn't raise the controller. During this distraction, I didn't notice Owen fly through the VOR and miss the turn for the approach. By the time I got him turned around, I had contacted the approach controller. By now our choices were Bombay and nothing but Bombay.

The heavy rain had driven away all the other air traffic. When I was able to raise Bombay Approach, he cleared us for vectors to a straight in. It was a localizer approach without a glidepath. The reported weather set the ceiling at 400 feet. I told Owen that we were going to land from this approach no matter what. There would be no overshoot. I think the concept of flying in actual bad weather was so strange to him that he accepted what I said. I told him to leave the autopilot on for the approach and just monitor the gauges. I monitored him.

The whine in the radio got worse. It was then that I realized that the noise was Owen humming nervously into the intercom.

We were flying in and out of rain showers, but the worst of the weather had passed. The autopilot flew the approach and we broke out with the runway ahead of us. It was covered with standing water, but Owen handled the landing well.

When he turned off onto a taxiway, the whine in the radios stopped.

It was well after midnight when they landed. At Bombay, there are terminal buildings on both sides of the airport, domestic and international. Charlie wanted the domestic side because he knew the international section shut down at that time of night. Despite his protests to the ground controller, the "Follow Me" jeep led them to the international side. The driver left before they could get the door open to talk to him.

The two pilots sat in the airplane, in the rain, waiting for a handler or anyone else to show up. No one did.

I called the ground controller and told him we wanted transportation to the domestic side and the hotel. He thought we needed customs. It was a long time before I convinced him to send the jeep back. Then we were forced to start up and follow the jeep to the other side of the field for parking. It was dark there too. It cost us a $40-bribe to convince the driver to give us a ride to the terminal building. There we tried to contact Air India to get a handler and fuel, but everyone was gone. We couldn't even get a taxi to the hotel. It was not very far off the airport, so we walked. It was three o'clock in the morning by the time we got to bed.

Wes McIntosh: Charlie (right) standing next to one of the new de Havilland Buffalos that he delivered to several air forces around the globe with Wes McIntosh (left).

Narsarssuak: Sugarloaf Mountain, a familiar landmark for international delivery pilots, guards the entrance to the fiord leading to Narsarssuak, Greenland.

Sri Lanka: (L-R, Joe Deluce, Anseim, Charlie, Weerakody) Canadian pilots Vaughn and Deluce relax in Crete with Sri Lankan Air Force pilots during enforced delayed delivery of Hawker Siddeley 748.

Thailand: This is one of the many de Havilland Dash 8s delivered by Charlie, pictured parked at Narsarssuak, Greenland, on the way to Thailand.

The Crash: In July, 1990, Charlie flew a temporarily repaired de Havilland Buffalo from Ecuador to Calgary, Alberta. The nose wheel folded back on landing which started a flash fire in the cockpit. The aircraft was destroyed.

Africa: Charlie delivered a de Havilland Buffalo to a remote part of Kenya for the United Nations in December, 1995. Charlie visited this local village while waiting for a ride out of the area.

Through Russia: (L-R, Mark Harper, Charlie) The two pilots are standing beside a Hawker Siddeley 748 at Manado, Indonesia, on their way from New Zealand to Whitehorse, Yukon.

We got up at eight in the morning, hoping for a full day's flying. We contacted a handler and wasted several hours trying to convince him and the airport bureaucrats that we had cleared customs in Calcutta. Then we found out that we could not get fuel until 17:30 that afternoon. That was hard to comprehend at a busy airport like that, but I believed it after waiting all day for the fuel truck to pull in front of the aircraft. Then they would only take cash for the fuel. I had left Canada with lots of U.S. dollars, but a week in Bangkok had put a hole in it and I knew I couldn't afford very many cash fuel stops.

We departed for Muscat, Oman, on the tip of the Arabian Peninsula after 18:00 that evening.

The weather to Muscat was good, but the headwind was strong. By the time we got there, it was dark, but not too late for a quick turnaround. The only problem at Muscat was that we had to pay cash for the fuel again.

During the takeoff roll at Muscat, the spoiler pressure light came on. Owen saw it and rejected the takeoff, which was the right thing to do. He pulled off the runway and declared that we would have to get it fixed. We cycled the spoilers and the light went out. I asked Owen to run the engines up. The light stayed out. Then I told him it was okay to depart. This suggestion unravelled all authority that I had accumulated with him. His by-the-book aviation experience had no room for such practical suggestions. He made the problem out to be really. It really wasn't. We departed against Owen's better judgement.

We flew a slow leg to Bahrain in the Persian Gulf against a headwind. The spoiler pressure light flickered on several times just to prove to Owen that he was right and we should have stopped. We stayed in Bahrain for two nights since it was after two o'clock in the morning before we got to bed on the first night. I needed the extra rest. I was tired of battling Owen, the headwinds, the bureaucrats, the aircraft snags and the clock.

Our next leg was to Luxor, Egypt. I expected a lot of problems there after giving them a hard time on my previous trip. We taxied to the ramp. The same hopeful handler from Egypt Air was there with his chocks waving us in. I directed Owen to park on the other side of the tarmac. The handler ran over. While Owen was shutting down, I opened the door and jumped out.

"We don't want handling," I yelled.

"Oh, yes. Must have handling," he said. Then he recognized me. "Oh yes, no handling."

"That's right; no handling."

He went away without any fuss. We processed through customs and the airport administration on our own with little trouble. It was the quickest turnaround I have ever had in Egypt.

September 25, 1993

It was exactly the opposite for Iraklion, Greece. On the way I battled headwinds, a spoiler pressure light and a rebellious copilot only to arrive just before the Prime Minister. Everything was screwed up. The Olympic Airways handler was not available, but we still had to pay for him. The hotels were all booked. We ended up spending a short night on the other side of town in a lousy hotel that took more of our cash.

September 26, 1993

I changed our plans. The snag list on the airplane was growing and it would be due for a 50-hour inspection before we completed the delivery. I decided to go to Innsbruck, Austria. It wasn't on our itinerary and it wasn't on our way, but Innsbruck was the maintenance base for Tyrolean Airlines, a Dash 8 operator. I had done deliveries for them and had become friends with Herman Winter, their chief maintenance engineer. I decided if we stopped there, we could get a growing list of snags fixed, wire for more cash and get caught up on sleep. When I mentioned fixing the airplane, Owen was all for it.

Flying direct to Innsbruck from Greece would have taken us over war-torn Yugoslavia. Instead, we took the long way up the east coast of Italy across the Adriatic Sea from Yugoslavia. The headwinds were still bad and we ended up landing at Venice, Italy, for fuel. It was a mistake. It cost us several hours and the rest of our cash. The fuel was expensive and they wouldn't take credit cards. I showed the fuel agent the rest of our American money and arranged for that much fuel. I figured it would be enough to get us to Innsbruck if our turn northbound resulted in less headwind.

The flight to Innsbruck was hell. We departed with the spoiler light on and marginal fuel. I had Yugoslavia on my right and Owen on my left. He was either arguing, humming or complaining. The headwind let up enough that I was able to convince myself and Owen that we could make it to Innsbruck. When we got there I found out that Herman Winter was out of town. I called his wife. She connected him with me. I explained our situation and he made a series of phone calls to authorize the maintenance.

Franz, the maintenance shop foreman looked the Dash 8 over. "Charlie, this airplane is scrap." "Scrap" wasn't the word he used, but it meant the same thing.

"Just fix the snags on the list, Franz," I said, "and let me know what else it needs."

They worked on it for one day and one night. When they were done, Franz admitted that the airplane looked worse than it was. "Ignore the spoiler pressure light," he said, "It's just a sensor problem, but don't fly into ice, Charlie. The boots are rotten. We started to patch them and then gave up."

On September 27, we departed late in the day for Glasgow, Scotland, where we stayed overnight. Catching up on some sleep helped ease the tension between Owen and me. We developed more of a truce than a friendship. The weather was good for the Atlantic crossing the next day but the headwinds were strong. We flew to Reykjavik for another overnight. From there, we stopped at Godthab in Greenland, Iqaluit, and Sept Iles. We were able to stay out of the clouds most of the time but couldn't dodge the headwinds. The silence in the cockpit made these legs seem even longer. Both of us just wanted to finish the trip and be done with each other.

After an overnight in Sept Iles, we flew to Bangor, Maine, for fuel and then on to our final destination, the Atlanta's Peachtree Falcon Airport.

I don't wish any man ill will, but I was happy to say goodbye to Owen and wish that I never had to fly with him again.

CHAPTER THIRTY-ONE

January, 1994 - Botswana

"Sometimes you take trips against your better judgement. You justify it in your own mind, but that doesn't make it a good idea."

Charlie Vaughn

𝕵anuary 12, 1994

Michael Bannock from World Wide Aircraft Ferry called to see if I would take a short flight in a de Havilland Buffalo with retired de Havilland pilot Mick Saunders. He needed the airplane delivered from Toronto Island Airport to Huron Airpark at Centralia, north of London, Ontario. It was a Mexican Navy airplane that was in Canada for overhaul. We would return in a Turbo-Beaver that was waiting to be flown back to Toronto.

It was a simple request: drive to Toronto; fly the Buffalo to Centralia; fly the Turbo-Beaver to Toronto; drive home. I agreed.

At the end of the conversation, Michael asked me if I would be interested in delivering a Cessna 337 from the United States to Botswana in southern Africa. There were 30 of them to go to different third world countries. He had all the pilot seats filled for an initial trip of three but was asking in case someone dropped out. I said, "Yes," meaning, "Yes I was interested." If asked to go, I would want to know more about the airplanes before agreeing to cross the Atlantic in one.

I told Robina I might be back in time for supper and I left for Toronto.

During the 30-minute flight to Centralia, Mick and I encountered a fuel transfer problem with the Buffalo. The Aero Support mechanics asked us to stay overnight while they worked on the airplane so we would be available to test fly it the next day.

January 13, 1994

The weather was bad. A cold northwest wind was blowing low cloud and snow flurries in from Lake Huron but the airplane was ready. We filed a roundtrip IFR flight plan to London, Ontario, just 22 nm to the southeast for the test flight. I rode in the left seat. We planned to fly an ILS approach at London to check the radios and then return to Centralia.

The radios worked fine, but as we were intercepting the localizer on final at London, the low oil pressure light came on for the right engine. We couldn't see oil leaking out of the engine and it seemed to be running fine. I didn't like to mess around with it at low altitude so I shut it down. The Buffalo has lots of horsepower on each side and we were lightly loaded so we elected to fly back to Centralia on one engine. There was no one in London who could fix a Buffalo, so it made sense to land where the mechanics were.

Like many of Canada's airports, Huron Airpark in Centralia, was built during World War II for the British Commonwealth Air Training Plan. The military continued to use it as an air base following the war. When CFB Centralia was finally decommissioned in the 1960s, the Ontario Development Corporation took over the old base, renamed it Huron Airpark and offered industry incentives to move in. The Aero Support overhaul centre occupied one of the large hangars, but the activity did not justify full-scale airport maintenance. Snow removal was limited to one runway.

The return to Centralia presented quite a challenge. Charlie had to land the 35,000-pound airplane on Runway 28. The pavement was icy; there was a strong, right crosswind; and the engine was shut down on the crosswind side. He would not be able to use reverse thrust and braking would be limited by the ice on the runway.

I knew we had plenty of room to modulate the brakes to keep the airplane straight and slow it down. The runway was 5,000-feet long. The approach went well. We touched down on the button of the runway and I started squeezing the brakes. They didn't work. At first I thought they were locked up on the ice, but they had failed completely. I was able to keep straight with the left engine, but we had to stop. I fired the nitrogen emergency brake system. It worked but it was a high-pucker-factor landing.

We left the airplane at Aero Support and returned to Toronto in the Turbo-Beaver without further incident. When we arrived, there was a message waiting for me to call World Wide. Michael Bannock's secretary, Angene Brown, said that my Cessna 337 trip to Botswana was on for January 17! I didn't know that I had a trip to Botswana. I started asking her a bunch of questions about the arrangements, most of which she couldn't answer. She said the airplanes were a gift from the Americans to Botswana. The south African country was going to use them to patrol game preserves in the fight against the poaching of elephants and rhinoceros. Angene didn't know any more except there was no one else to take the trip.

Well, you don't shoot the messenger. Michael was away. The humanitarian aspect of the delivery appealed to me and I had never been to Botswana. I said that I'd go.

Barry Morris was one of the other pilots. We met in Toronto and rode the airlines to Philadelphia together. Barry told me that the airplanes were ex-navy Cessna 0-2As, the military version of the Cessna 337.

In Philadelphia we drove a rental car to Middletown, Delaware, where the airplanes were being readied for the trip by Summit Aviation.

For Barry Morris, the flight was a significant milestone in his life. Just six months before he had been badly injured in an aircraft accident. He had been riding in an ultralight as a passenger when the pilot lost control on takeoff. The aircraft stalled at low altitude and pitched to the ground. At first, it appeared that Barry's flying days were over, but he recovered quickly and worked hard on rehabilitation. By the end of the year, he was back in the air, but the flight to Botswana was to be the supreme test of whether his injuries had permanently affected his usefulness as a commercial pilot.

The Cessna 337 "Skymaster" was a high-wing, four-to-six-place, light aircraft with an unusual twin-engine, centreline thrust configuration. Designed in 1960, the airplane was powered by two Continental 210-horsepower engines; one in the nose, and one in the rear fuselage between a twin-boom tail.

The 0-2 military version of the aircraft was essentially the same as the civilian. Cessna Aircraft delivered 500 0-2s to the United States Air Force during the late 1960s. Most were 0-2As, designated as forward air controller aircraft. Many were used for visual reconnaissance, target identification and air-ground coordination in Vietnam. Their equipment included underwing pylons for external stores such as rockets, flares and 7.62 mm gun packs.

Charlie had been in a Cessna 337 once before. He had flown a demonstration tour to Newfoundland in a new one for Leavens Brothers sixteen years earlier. He and Barrie hoped to do a test/familiarization flight in Middletown before departing on the trip. When they arrived the clouds were too low for a visual flight, but that wasn't the only problem. The three 0-2s were parked outside and, like the entire airport, they were covered in a thick layer of ice. One of them was missing a propeller.

The people at Summit told Charlie and Morris that the 0-2s had been in desert storage for an indeterminate number of years. The airplanes were complete except for the passenger seats that had been taken out to make room for temporary cabin fuel tanks. There was a good compliment of radios in each one but no autopilots. The armament activation systems were still there but the gun pylons had been removed. They did not have airframe de-icing equipment.

The airplanes carried United States Navy markings and were still military property. This meant that only certain airports around the world were available for fuel stops. Many countries did not welcome what would appear to be American military presence, no matter how small. The trip had been arranged through diplomatic channels. A 72-hour time window had been established for each of the stops and the clock was already ticking.

It added up to a difficult ferry trip. If I had been asked to do the delivery with the knowledge I had standing beside the aircraft, I would have declined. But you don't abandon aircraft if you have any loyalty to your ferry company. There was still the humanitarian aspect of the delivery and I still had never been to Botswana. Summit pulled the aircraft into the hangar to melt the ice. We used the time to load our gear and get familiar with the 0-2A.

There was more bad news. The third pilot was supposed to be Bill Loverseed, but he had been delayed in the Azores where strong headwinds prevented him from flying a Twin Otter directly to Florida. He sent a message that he was taking the long way around the top of the Atlantic and would be late.

The next day Barry and I punched through the persistent overcast and flew IFR to Bangor, Maine. We left Bill the airplane that was waiting for a new prop figuring he would catch up while we were having our ferry tanks installed in Maine. He did, three days later. It took one more day to have his aircraft fitted with tanks.

The U.S. Navy required us to fax a progress report every morning and night through Summit Aviation in New Jersey. On January 23, we faxed that we were flight planned VFR to St. John's, Newfoundland, and asked them to reset the diplomatic clock.

Bill led the first leg and handled the air traffic control communications. The weather was good so we flew about a quarter of a mile apart, keeping each other in sight. We tuned our radios to a common, unused frequency. We all had portable GPSs, so if one of us lost sight of the other two, we would radio our GPS distance to the next waypoint. By comparing the responses, we could tell our distance apart. It was comforting to be with other aircraft, but it was more work keeping track of each other than flying alone.

January 25, 1994

We lost a day in St. John's waiting for bad weather to clear. On January 25, we departed southeastbound; destination, the Azores, the Portuguese islands three quarters of the way across the Atlantic.

One hundred miles out of Newfoundland, we encountered heavy cloud and ice. We fanned out to maintain separation and descended. At 3,000 feet above the sea, the ice started to melt. We levelled off. The flying was a challenge. We were hand-flying in cloud at low level while watching for ice, maintaining separation by exchanging GPS readouts over the communications radio, and juggling the fuel. It didn't leave much time for anything else.

The cabin fuel tanks installed for the trip were connected to the aircraft's regular fuel system via a "T" fitting in the cabin wall. The ferry tanks doubled the aircraft's fuel capacity for a total range of about 14 hours at a medium cruise speed of 150 knots.

To access the extra fuel, the pilots flew for awhile and then turned on a pair of electric fuel pumps on the cabin floor to transfer replacement fuel. They logged the transferred fuel to keep track of the quantity used. A flexible tube running to an elbow rigged in a side window vent provided positive air pressure for the ferry tanks.

At 200 miles out, the fuel gauges in my aircraft showed a decreasing quantity even though I had the transfer pumps on. The circuit breakers were all in. I reached behind me and could feel the pumps were running, but the fuel was not being transferred. It didn't figure. I was getting a little desperate. I had to find the problem soon or turn around before the wing tanks were half empty. To continue would have meant ditching in the North Atlantic if I couldn't get the cabin fuel into the airplane's system.

I reached back one more time and with some difficulty, pulled the ferry tank fuel cap off. There was a "whoosh" and a "bang" as air rushed into the tanks and popped their sides. Ice must have been blocking the vent line elbow where it went through the window. I warned the two other pilots about my problem but they said that they weren't having the same trouble. I left the cabin tank cap ajar for the rest of the flight. From then on, the ferry fuel transferred into the wings without any difficulty.

Nine hours and five minutes after departing St. John's, the three Cessnas arrived at Santa Maria, on the Azores.

We landed in single file about 30 minutes after dark. The airport administrator welcomed us with a $58 landing fee and a $200 fee for the lights, each. We tried to talk him down since we had arrived together, but it didn't do us any good.

On the ground, Charlie checked the cabin fuel vent system again and found nothing wrong. Close examination of all the aircraft revealed that the elbow rigged in his side window had a relief hole drilled in the back of it and the others didn't. Charlie could only speculate that the venturi effect of his setup had dropped the temperature in the vent tube and ice had formed where the tube joined the elbow going into the tank. He would never know since the rest of the trip was flown in increasingly warmer air.

January 26, 1994

The next day we departed for Dakar, Senegal. Dakar sits on the most Western point of Africa's hip before the continent curves back in. This leg was also entirely over open water but it was a lot easier to fly than the previous one. The weather was good so we could keep each other in sight easily and didn't have to constantly exchange radio position updates.

About 150 miles from Dakar, I was beginning to think the radio had been quiet for too long. I could see Bill up ahead, but Barrie was not in sight. I was about to call the other pilots when Barrie came on the frequency and said, "Hey guys; I just had a total electric failure!"

It was obvious that he had restored his power or he couldn't have talked to us. His GPS position indicated he was behind so we slowed down to allow him to catch up. He tucked in between Bill and I and stayed there for the rest of the flight.

A total electric failure is a scary prospect in an 0-2. The entire airplane is electric: gyro instruments, cowl flaps, landing gear, wing flaps and armament. Everything but the compass runs off a single 60-amp electric system. His engines had continued to run, but they would not have run long. We were using electric pumps to transfer ferry fuel to the wings.

Barrie closed up on our formation and pumped fuel into the wings every few minutes. He told us that he had used the generator on the tachometer to excite the alternator fields and that had restored his electric power. It remained on for the rest of the leg.

Approaching Dakar, we could see the African coastline. It was a welcome sight. We had been in the air over 10 hours. As we got closer, the visibility dropped steadily in a thick heat haze. The air traffic controller cleared each one of us for a full ILS approach. Then he announced that the localizer was out of service. We used the GPSs to fly straight in. Once we were lined up, we could see the runway.

After Barrie shut down, he tried a starter. Nothing. The aircraft's battery seemed to be dead. We were all pretty tired, so we buttoned the aircraft up for the night and headed for the hotel that was attached right to the terminal building.

That evening, we faxed the Navy through Summit Aviation and told them our problem. The reply was just, "Stay together and advise."

We started troubleshooting the problem with Barrie's aircraft. While we were working on it, an American came over and asked if he could help. Jim Lowenbauer was a civilian employed by Beechcraft assigned to maintain a Beech King

Air for the U.S. Department of Defense in Senegal. It didn't take him long to find a blown shunt, the main fuse for the electric system. We faxed Summit on Jim's machine and asked them to send us another shunt. They replied that they didn't have one and that it would take a few days to find one and ship it over.

The three pilots didn't want to wait in Dakar if they could help it. The city of one and a half million people was hot, dirty and poor. They had encountered those conditions before, but Dakar was exceptionally bad. The beggars included hungry children with running sores on their skin. They waited in front of the hotel and pleaded for the chance to carry a bag, or do anything, for a coin. The rooms were not air conditioned. The tub in Charlie's room was so crusted with fungus that he didn't dare take a bath. There were better hotels downtown, but the trio didn't think Dakar was the kind of place to leave three aircraft parked on the ramp unattended for long. They decided to stay close to the airport.

The next day I took the burned out shunt to the Air Senegal maintenance shop. It was a primitive facility. I had better tools in my portable kit than they were using in the hangar, but the native mechanic tried to be helpful. We found a piece of copper and a small strand of silver solder. I cut and filed the copper until I was satisfied that, at least visually, it was the same size as the old one. I could only hope that the resistance of the material was similar. The shop had an oxy/acetylene torch. The regulator was broken, so the mixture came out full blast. They didn't have an igniter, so we built a small paper fire on the cement floor. I lit the torch from that. It was a one-shot deal. I laid pieces of silver solder at the joints and carefully waved the roaring torch over the part. It worked.

Before they tried the barnyard repair in the aircraft, the three pilots traced through the electric system to see if they could find what had caused the shunt to blow. Charlie discovered the problem in the circuit breaker panel. To connect the ferry fuel pumps to the electric system, the installer had run the wire through the front of the circuit panel and then held it in place by snapping the face plate back on. The cover had chafed through the coating on the wire and shorted it out. Since it was connected to the electric system after a circuit breaker, it blew the main shunt. Charlie didn't have anything nice to say about the workmanship.

Charlie checked and found the same problem on the other two aircraft. The trio rewired the pumps on all three and tested the shunt on Barrie's aircraft. It worked. They faxed Summit and asked them to cancel the part order and to reset the diplomatic clock. They planned to depart the next day. That night, Jim Lowenbauer took them to his resort hotel on the other side of town for their first proper meal in three days.

January 29, 1994

We took off for Abidjan, the capital of Ivory Coast. We flew direct, heading inland. There were no clouds, but a yellow haze reduced visibility. When we levelled off at 10,000 feet, I could smell smoke. This really bothered me after seeing the wiring problems on the airplanes. I radioed the other guys. They were smelling it too, which was good news. It was coming from outside the aircraft.

The smoke was the yellow haze that clouded the horizon. The Senegalese were burning scrub off the arid land in an effort to expand their agriculture. The three pilots were happy to leave the blackened landscape. When they crossed over the mountains in bordering Guinea, the visibility cleared and lush valleys stretched before them. The greenery followed them all the way to the Ivory Coast.

They stayed overnight in Abidjan where Charlie had his first real bath in four days. The next day they struck out across the Bay of Guinea directly for Port Gentil, Gabon, the most westerly part of Africa.

The next leg out of Gabon was made difficult by the diplomacy involved in delivering an American military aircraft. The three pilots were required to remain clear of both Congo and Angola airspace, which meant staying at least 200 miles out to sea. Their first available stop was Windhoek in Namibia, the former Southwest Africa. It was 1,600 nm away. To land anywhere in between would risk losing the aircraft, being fined, imprisoned, or even being shot down.

There was no weather information available along the way. We could not carry enough fuel to make Windhoek against much headwind. The only thing we could do was take off and monitor the GPS ground speed. If it was good, we would continue; if not, we'd have to turn back and try it again on a different day.

Flying close to a war zone made us nervous so we changed the aircraft registration on our flight plan. Up to that point we had been using "Navy 068 plus two." For this leg, we called ourselves "November Alpha 068 plus two."

Our flight plan indicated that we would stay outside Angolan airspace but Bill called Angola Control just to let them know we were there and remaining clear.

"Angola Control, this is November Alpha 068 plus two. Be advised that we are at the northern boundary of your airspace, remaining clear 200 miles to the west."

"Navy 068, Angola, roger, I check that, thanks for the call."

The GPS made it easy to stay outside the 200 nautical mile limit but we kept looking over our left shoulder for fighter activity. We never saw any.

The trio were riding a tailwind most of the way. They left Angola behind with fuel to spare and turned inland. They were greeted with the bleak coastline of Namibia's Namib Desert. They continued into the mountains and landed at Windhoek, 11.3 hours after departing Gabon.

Windhoek is an oasis at the 6,000-foot level in the middle of an arid range of mountains in an arid land. The three pilots stayed the night, sleeping late into the next morning for the first time since leaving home.

Hand flying a one-man airplane on long legs like that really takes a lot out of you. I knew how tired I was; Barrie must have been ready to pass out. He looked pretty pale each time he got out of the airplane, but he made it.

The next day it was just a four-hour hop over to Gaborone in Botswana. Since Windhoek is a mountain airport with a permanent high density altitude, we filled our wing tanks only.

All three pilots had to nurse their airplanes into the air after using most of Windhoek's runway. They milked the necessary altitude out of the thin, hot air to clear the rest of the mountains.

East of Windhoek, the high terrain fell away to the Kalahari Desert. The trio flew over some of the herds of wildlife that the airplanes they were delivering were going to protect.

When Bill called Gaborone Approach, the controller said that they wanted us to fly over to the military airport and not the International Airport as planned. The air base wasn't marked on our charts but he gave us the coordinates which, when plugged into our GPSs, gave the heading and distance. The visibility was good and pretty soon we could see the airport.

The American gift of the old Cessnas was a big deal to Botswana. A contingent of government officials was waiting in the afternoon heat for their arrival.

We met the officials as well as some of the pilots and mechanics who were going to be working on the airplanes. I don't know how the O-2s will last very long. We had more tools in our emergency kits than they had total. The African mechanic who removed the ferry tank fittings from my aircraft cross threaded the connection to the wing tank when he tried to put the plug in. So there he was, trying to thread the plug while high octane avgas poured down his arm. I managed to do it for him, but not before we were both soaked in fuel. That is not fun on a hot day.

Bill, Barrie and I packed the ferry tank fittings into our luggage and bid goodbye to Botswana. There were other 0-2s to be ferried there, but I told Michael Bannock that I was not interested. He mentioned there might also be 0-2s to go to Mali, south of Morocco. I had never been to Mali. I told him to let me know.

CHAPTER THIRTY-TWO

February, 1995 - Simon says

"Some ferry flights go smoothly. This was not one of them."

Charlie Vaughn

Michael Bannock called and asked if I could find a copilot and deliver a Jetstream 31 from Peterborough, Ontario, to Prestwick, Scotland. It was an ex-Canadian Partner airplane that aircraft broker Floyd Carson had sold to Korea. It was going to Vietnam after some work was done on it in the U.K.

I had never flown a 31 before so I said, "Yes." I figured I could find an experienced Jetstream pilot to go with me. The airplane requires two qualified pilots. It has always been my interpretation of the regulations requiring two pilots that one pilot certified on the airplane could flight train another pilot as long as there were no passengers. I don't think it says anywhere that the flight can't be halfway around the world.

I phoned Hans Grob in Hamilton. He said he wasn't available but suggested I call Simon Austin, a young ex-Canadian Partner airline pilot who had been laid off when the company sold the very aircraft I had been asked to deliver.

Simon Austin turned out to be a good find. He didn't have any international ferry experience, but he knew the airplane well, was a good pilot and was a nice guy to boot. He was happy to have the work. The airplane was another story.

Charlie borrowed a set of operating handbooks for the airplane and its Garrett engines from Hans Grob and learned what he could during the two days before his scheduled departure.

I met Simon in Toronto. We planned to pick the Jetstream up in Peterborough, test fly it locally and then hop over to Toronto before setting out eastbound the next day. When we got to the Flying Colours paint shop in Peterborough, the airplane wasn't ready. We waited until they pushed it out of the hangar, but by then the weather had come down. We ground ran the airplane and found that there was no prop deice and the cabin pressure wouldn't come up. There were several other minor snags, so we waited until the next day for better weather and then flew to Toronto International for repairs.

Charlie didn't think it would take long to fix the airplane in Toronto, so before going home that night, he "installed" a GPS antenna on the cabin roof above the airstair door and ran a lead-in cable to the cockpit. It would be five days before the airplane was ready.

While the Jetstream was sitting in the hangar at Toronto, a Transport Canada inspector spotted my antenna. He couldn't miss it. I had taped it on with that silver-backed high-speed tape. He took photos of my non-standard installation and phoned me at home. He said that the antenna was an unapproved installation by an unqualified person and that I would be charged. I told him I would take it off, which I did the next day in Toronto. I taped the antenna to the inside of the windshield which worked, but not as well.

When the airplane was ready, Charlie met Austin in Toronto again. The cabin pressure problem was related to the overinflation of the nose oleo. The paint shop people had pumped it up in order to fit the vertical tail into their low hangar opening. The extra extension prevented the squat switch from working and the pressurization would not activate.

We started out early enough to make Goose Bay, Labrador, with a fuel stop at Sept Iles, Quebec. We leap frogged over a freezing rain storm that was approaching

Sept Iles. It looked like a quick turnaround would keep us ahead of the bad weather. When we got out of the airplane for the refuelling, we could see hydraulic fluid leaking along the left side of the fuselage and dripping off the tail cone. It looked like a don't-go-any-further-until-you-check-this-one-out problem.

An iron ore company maintained an aircraft mechanic and hangar on the airport. The mechanic agreed to put the Jetstream inside for $200 and work on it for so much per hour, as long as we paid him in cash. I didn't have much Canadian money, but I told him I would get more from a bank machine in town. He agreed. We moved it inside and he started removing panels. I tried to call flight service for an update on the approaching weather but the long distance lines serving Sept Iles were dead. I found out later that there had been a fire in the telephone switching station. Simon and I called a taxi and went into town.

The banking machines didn't work because they relied on telephone lines. I had American money but I knew we would need it later in the trip. We had supper and went back out to the airport.

The mechanic worked through the evening. The leak was coming from the hydraulic reservoir in the fuselage behind the base of the left wing. The mechanic said he found a loose fitting. He tightened it and started putting the airplane back together. It was late and the bad weather had caught up to us so we stayed the night.

The long distance phone lines were still dead in the morning but we were told they would be restored soon. The weather was still bad and I had no way to file a flight plan. The bill for the airplane was $600. I decided to wait.

We were in a time squeeze because it was a Thursday. I knew there was no access to Greenland on the weekends. The airports in Greenland are totally shutdown on Saturdays and Sundays. There is no air traffic control, crash/fire/rescue service, fuel or customs. Everything is locked up until Monday. The only way to get access to the big island on the weekend is to pay overtime fees for all those services. I knew that wasn't in Michael Bannock's budget.

It was noon before the phone lines were reactivated. We got our money and rushed to the airport. Simon and I split up the work of checking weather, filing a flight plan, buying fuel, loading up all the hydraulic fluid available on the airport and paying our bill. We were airborne in record time. We could still make Greenland on what was left of Friday if we got a quick refuelling at Goose Bay, Labrador.

We flew over the now-familiar front and landed in Goose Bay. When we stepped out of the airplane, we could see a stream of hydraulic fluid running down the left side of the fuselage. There comes a time to stop pushing. This was one of those times. We let our Greenland window close and resigned ourselves to stay in Happy Valley, the town near the airport for the weekend.

We found a mechanic to work on the Jetstream. He accessed the hydraulic reservoir, but couldn't find the source of the leak. We were able to estimate our rate of hydraulic fluid loss from Sept Iles. We still had a better hydraulic loss range than fuel range, so I decided we could live with it.

Monday morning we departed early with full fuel, a full hydraulic fluid reservoir and all the spare hydraulic fluid in Goose. We stopped in Narsarssuak, Greenland, for fuel and a fluid top-up.

We flew to Reykjavik, Iceland, and stayed overnight. Sven Bjornson rounded us up more hydraulic fluid.

The final destination for the ferry flight was Prestwick, but the delivery contract included a four-day stop in East Midlands Airport in England where the Jetstream was scheduled for mandatory modification work before being taken to the British Aerospace factory in Prestwick. From Prestwick, it was going to be delivered to Seoul, Korea, by a Korean crew.

With the 31's short range, Charlie planned to stop in Glasgow for fuel before flying on to East Midlands, but when they were airborne on Tuesday, a strong tailwind gave them a ground speed that allowed them to change the destination all the way to East Midlands.

It turned out that Floyd Carson's maintenance representative at the modification shop was a retired Transport Canada airworthiness inspector from Toronto. During our conversations about the snags on the airplane, I mentioned the pending GPS antenna violation with his former inspector buddies back in Toronto. He said to leave that with him.

Michael Bannock had arranged for us to stay in East Midlands, which was not an exciting prospect. I found out the same money would buy Simon and me return air fares to Edinburgh where I knew we could stay with my friends Ian and Maureen Bishop. I asked Simon if he would like to see some of Scotland and he said, "Yes". The Bishops treated us to their naturally warm hospitality and introduced Simon to the best Scotch malts.

When we got back to the East Midlands airport, the maintenance people told us they had replaced a cracked hydraulic line under the reservoir. That had cured the leak. The ex-Transport Canada inspector said that he had telephoned his buddies back in Toronto and chewed them out for having nothing better to do than to force a pilot planning a flight across the North Atlantic to remove his practical but illegal antenna installation and place it inside the cockpit with an illegal, impractical installation. He told me that he didn't think I would hear about the incident again. I haven't - yet.

CHAPTER THIRTY-THREE

March, 1995 - Mcdougall again

"These were short trips, but they were interesting for a couple of different reasons."

Charlie Vaughn

Michael Bannock asked me to deliver a de Havilland Dash 8 from Wichita, Kansas, to Harrisburg, Pennsylvania. The airplane had been sold. It would be flown by a different crew from Washington, D.C., to Wichita. Washington is only 20 minutes by Dash 8 to Harrisburg, but by completing the transaction in Kansas, the purchaser saved enough taxes to justify hiring a ferry crew, obtaining a flight permit and returning the aircraft back across the country.

I asked Michael who the co-pilot would be.

"Owen Mcdougall," he said and then before I could reply, he added quickly, "He's a changed man, Charlie. Everybody says he is a different pilot since that flight from Bangkok with you."

I pride myself in being able to get along with most people, but that flight had been the only time that I wanted to dump a co-pilot enroute and Michael knew it. I had told him to never book me with Owen again.

"I don't have anyone else to fly with you," Michael said.

I let him talk me into it against my better judgement. "I guess I can stand him for a few hours," I replied.

"You won't regret it, this time," Michael said. He was right.

I met Owen in Toronto and we rode on the airlines together to Wichita. I told him right off. "I hope things go better on this trip than the last one."

"Charlie," he replied, "I hope you can forget the last one."

We were to pick the airplane up by 13:00 local time that day. We made it with an hour to spare, but the Dash 8 was not there. I called back to World Wide and was told to wait. Two hours later, the airplane arrived, but we had to wait for word of the transaction before departing. I used the time to ask the other pilots if there were any snags. There weren't. The transaction went through, but we had to wait for the ferry permit. It was nearly five o'clock before we had everything we needed.

On the flight back, the weather was good and so was Owen. I told him so.

April, 1995

Michael called and asked if I would do another Dash 8 transaction flight on April 19. This time it would be with Mick Saunders and we would do both legs of the delivery: Springfield, Missouri, to Pittsburg, Kansas, wait, and then fly it to Calgary, Alberta. I enjoyed those short flights when I could get back home on the same day.

At Springfield, the airplane was ready to go from World Wide Aircraft Sales (no relation to World Wide Aircraft Ferry) but we were told to wait by Jim Maclean. I knew Jim from previous deliveries.

"There's a delay getting a ferry permit for that airplane from Oklahoma City," he said, "It seems that someone blew up the Federal Building there."

"I've heard a lot of excuses in this business, Jim," I said, "but that one is a first."

The permit came through another FAA office shortly and we departed for Kansas. When we got there, we were told that the Federal Building had indeed been blown up and there would be no ferry permit to continue the flight. We stayed there overnight and saw the news coverage of the sabotaged building.

The next day, a permit arrived and we were on our way, but I hadn't heard the last of this one. They lost so many records in that blast, that I was contacted several months later and asked to swear an affidavit that I had indeed done that flight.

CHAPTER THIRTY-FOUR

June, 1995 - Grecian heat

*"We decided that the three airplanes were airworthy
enough to fly them out of Greece, but I wouldn't have
tried crossing the Atlantic in any one of them."*
Charlie Vaughn

$\mathfrak{M}$ichael Bannock asked me to go to Greece as one of the pilots to pick up three Canadian registered Piper Cheyenne IIs. They had been leased from Rocky Mountain Aircraft of Calgary, Alberta, for cloud seeding but no lease payments had been made on them for two years. Rocky Mountain wanted them back. The three airplanes were to be flown to Calgary together with one pilot in each. The other two pilots were Willi Ebner and Brent Souter.

I talked to Willi and found out that he and Bill Loverseed had tried to bring out two of these aircraft the year before. They had just taken off when they were called back. They were told on the radio that if they did not turn around, fighter aircraft would be dispatched. They obeyed and spent some time in custody before being released without the aircraft.

Michael Bannock assured me that this time all the export arrangements had been made and there would be no trouble. I didn't want to see the inside of a Greek jail, but it did sound like a challenge. I agreed to go.

A Canadian ferry permit had been issued for each airplane on the strength of a Greek Certificate of Airworthiness inspection. They were in rough shape. I don't think a mechanic had looked at them. They had been baking in the famous Greek sunshine for two years except for their one brief flight a year ago. The batteries were flat, most of the radios didn't work, all of the rubber, such as door seals and wing boots were cooked and rotten, none of the heaters worked and they were full of bird nests. We had time to work on them because the Greek government officials wouldn't let us take the airplanes. They said we didn't have the proper custom export permits.

The three of us worked on those airplanes outside on the ramp in the heat of the Grecian summer for five days. There were few facilities at the Thessaloniki Airport and no one in Greece seemed to know anything about Cheyennes. We used what tools I had brought with me and anything we could beg and borrow. Working outside on the ramp in the relentless hot sun was brutal but this was partly compensated for by the hotel accommodations. We were staying at the Sani Beach Hotel, a luxurious resort a fair distance south of the airport. We rented a car to run back and forth. At the end of each day we soaked in the baths in our rooms to cool off.

The constant exposure to heat and sun took its toll. On the fifth day, Charlie had to see the hotel doctor. He was suffering from sun stroke and dehydration. He was given water pills and told to stay in his hotel room. He spent two days recovering and waiting for the airplanes to be released.

Each day we were there, the customs officials said that we had to wait for a release that would "come soon". When I had recovered, we decided that the three airplanes were airworthy enough to get them out of Greece if we could get permission, but I wouldn't have tried crossing the Atlantic in any of them. We couldn't get Brent's Cheyenne to pressurize and none of the navigation radios worked in Willi's.

On the day we received permission to go, a truck showed up with a load of boxes that supposedly contained cloud seeding equipment and spare parts belonging to Rocky Mountain. We hadn't been told about them and there was no manifest. The boxes were taped up and unmarked. We wanted to get out of there before anyone changed their mind so we loaded up without taking the time to check what was in the boxes.

The weather was not great, but Willi got his GPS working, so we departed anyway. I knew Tulip Air in Rotterdam,

Holland, operated Cheyennes. We flew IFR to Rotterdam with a fuel stop in Venice, Italy.

Tulip Air worked on the airplanes for two days while we rested from our week-long ordeal in the heat.

After a fuel stop in Glasgow, we flew to Reykjavik, Iceland. Here we had to wait two more days because it was a weekend and Greenland was closed. We planned to rest here too, but it was the 40th anniversary of Iceland's independence from Denmark, so we joined the celebrations. There were no hotel rooms available because the Icelanders from the outlying areas had come to town for the festivities. Sven Bjornson from the fixed base operation arranged for us to stay in the university dormitory. Brent proved himself on this part of the trip. He was a good looking young guy and managed to find a good looking young girl with a car who took us all to the best restaurants and free beer spots in Reykjavik.

On Monday, June 19, we departed on a marathon day to Sondre Strom, Greenland, Iqaluit, Northwest Territories and Churchill, Manitoba. Our total flying time was nine hours. We had wanted to stop overnight in Iqaluit, but when we landed there, we discovered that Canadian Prime Minister Jean Chretien was visiting with German Chancellor Helmut Kohl and the town's accommodations were filled. The weather was good and the June daylight went right around the clock, so we decided to keep going. Canada customs looked at the cargo without opening any of it and gave us a temporary entry permit on the condition that we would clear permanently at Calgary International Airport.

On the non-stop flight from Churchill to Calgary, Brent was trailing the furthest behind. He received a message from Rocky Mountain Aircraft through the La Ronge Flight Service Station. "Land at Rocky Mountain's home base at Springbank Airport on the other side of Calgary from the International Airport."

He didn't want to get into a message war with Rocky Mountain, so he replied that he couldn't make them out and changed frequencies. We didn't change our destination.

When we landed at Calgary International, we were greeted by several customs officers and their dog. They impounded the aircraft until they could sort out what was in the boxes. We never heard that it wasn't aircraft parts. The officers were not happy when we told them we didn't know what they contained. They questioned us and then let us go.

I saw the other two off to Toronto and then went to visit my son Dennis in Calgary. It was three days before I felt well enough to travel home.

I wouldn't say I was too old to fly those trips, but I am past the time I can spend five days on the ramp in the Grecian heat without ill effect.

CHAPTER THIRTY-FIVE

December, 1995
Bad attitude to Kenya

"Delivering a well-used Buffalo half way around the world is difficult enough without putting up with a copilot who has an attitude problem."

Charlie Vaughn

𝕵n September, 1995, I went to Centralia with Michael Bannock to ground run a de Havilland Buffalo in anticipation of flying it to Kenya in east central Africa. It was an ex-Omani Air Force airplane that had been leased to the United Nations to support the peacekeeping efforts in neighbouring Sudan. Aero Support in Centralia had been contracted to make some repairs, paint the Buffalo white and add the UN markings.

Our ground run was to determine the snags before the airplane went into the shop. The worst problem was the left engine which flamed out on its own for no apparent reason. I handed the engineers a list of problems and expected a call to go in a few weeks. I had just about given up when I received an urgent call mid-afternoon on November 29, three months later. "Could you drive to Centralia immediately to depart on the trip to Kenya?" The Buffalo was finally fixed and a United Nations pilot and mechanic were there ready to go as soon as I arrived. I said that I would leave shortly.

I called my nephew who lives nearby and asked him to drive me so my car would not be stuck in Centralia. I threw some clothes in a bag, grabbed my trip kit and left. We had a flat tire on the way. The spare was no good and we wasted a lot of time waiting for a service truck. By the time I arrived at Aero Support's hangar, the crew had given up on the idea of departing that day and had gone back to their hotel room in London, Ontario. It was a bad start to a troublesome trip.

The UN pilot was Murray Clarkin, a New Zealander who had been contracted by the leasing company to fly the Buffalo to Kenya and operate it there. Another pilot would fly with Clarkin in Kenya.

The mechanic contracted by the leasing company was Ron Edwards, a Canadian recently retired from the Canadian Armed Forces.

Charlie met the two men at the hotel. Clarkin was pleasant enough but was obviously miffed that Charlie was late. He said that he had test flown the airplane and declared it ready. He suggested that he start the trip in the left seat, since he knew the airplane. Charlie readily agreed.

Since Charlie's experience flying a Dash 8 back to North America from Thailand with the "copilot from hell," he preferred the right seat when starting out with a pilot for the first time. His theory was that it was easier to monitor the other pilot's performance without being busy flying the airplane himself.

Charlie couldn't believe the cabin load in the Buffalo when he saw it. The leasing company had arranged to take tools and spare parts as well as a full range of everything that might be needed but could not be bought in the African bush. The camping gear included an all-terrain four-wheeler that had been driven up the rear loading ramp into the Buffalo's military-style cabin.

The one thing that Murray didn't have was food for the flight. I went to the corner store in Centralia while the loading was being finished. There was not enough jet fuel available in Centralia to fill the Buffalo so the first stop was to be the London Airport, ten minutes away.

On takeoff, the landing gear wouldn't retract. Murray circled while I checked a few things with Ron Edward's help. We couldn't get it to work, so we landed back at Centralia. The maintenance engineers at Aero Support said the airplane was too heavily loaded to jack up for a gear swing. We went flying with the mechanics on board but they couldn't find the problem either.

There was nothing else we could do except push the Buffalo into the hangar and unload the mountain of cargo. When we had done that, the mechanics found a corroded cannon plug leading to the squat switch on the nose gear. The day was shot by the time we loaded everything again.

We departed early December 1 for St. John's Newfoundland. We flew through a warm front with snow and freezing rain. The crew oxygen cylinders were empty, so we had to stay in the soup below 10,000 feet. The de-icing and radio equipment all worked which was a bonus when delivering used airplanes. Murray handled the Buffalo very well and showed little of the bad attitude that was to surface all too soon.

We landed at St. John's after five hours in the air. The bad weather followed us in, so we arranged for hangar storage overnight. We were also able to have the oxygen tanks filled.

The delivery flight was being handled by World Wide Aircraft Ferrying which was to have arranged for pre-paid fuel, accommodations and overflight clearances. The fact that the crew had lost nearly two days from the start made it difficult to keep these arrangements on schedule.

When they landed at St. John's, they discovered that fuel had not been prepaid for them, there were no hotel reservations and the rescheduled overflight clearances had not been forwarded. Clarkin flew off the handle. He started ranting about what a lousy outfit World Wide was and wanted to know how they were supposed to fly to Africa without support.

His complaining was out of place. The refueller was happy to fill up the Buffalo on a credit card; I telephoned downtown and found that there were hotel rooms available. I knew we didn't need the overflight clearances until Africa. I didn't respond to Murray's tirade, but I decided he either had never flown internationally or he had a bad attitude problem. That night some of our overflight clearances and refuelling confirmations arrived at the hotel by fax.

We got up early the next morning to make up for some lost time.

Murray was still surly but he settled down in the cockpit for the flight to Ponta Delgada in the Azores. I worked the radios. The weather had improved and we picked up a good tailwind which made him almost happy. We flew straight across the Atlantic at 9,000 feet so we wouldn't have to wear oxygen masks. The Azores came into sight less than six hours from St. John's.

I received a clearance to descend toward Ponta Delgada. Through 5,000 feet, the left engine start light came on. The Buffalo Operating Manual calls for an immediate shut down of the engine if this happens in flight. If the starter engages into a running engine, it could destroy itself. Murray shut the engine down calmly and systematically. I told the control tower of our situation and said that it was not an emergency. We landed without a problem.

The cargo manifest indicated that the Buffalo contained a spare bleed air start valve. While Ron Edwards pulled the left cowlings off and removed the old valve, Clarkin and Charlie dug through the mountains of spare part boxes. It took a long time but they found the replacement they needed. Edwards installed the new valve and replaced the cowlings. By the time the crew finished the paperwork for the Portuguese airport authorities, arranged for fuel, grabbed some supper and went to bed, it was a short night.

Their next destination was Palma on the Spanish island of Majorca in the Mediterranean, 1,300 nm to the east. They had a good tailwind again and had the airport in sight in six hours.

Descending through 5,000 feet, the left engine start light came on.

As soon as I called it out, Ron came forward and told Murray not to shut the engine down. "It has to be in the sensor," he said, "There is nothing wrong with the bleed air valve."

There was some discussion, but Murray went along with him and we landed without any trouble. Ron immediately started to work on the left engine. Murray was antsy to get going. He wanted to put in another leg before calling it a day.

The refueller said he had no knowledge of prepaid fuel for us.

Murray went nuts. He started yelling to anyone who would listen.

It didn't do any good. The ground crew spoke very little English and understood even less. It was Sunday and the refueller's office was closed. There was no way to get confirmation that we had prepaid, but Murray would not be pacified. I ignored him. I went to the terminal building and changed $1,500 into local currency. It was enough for 5,000 litres. The Buffalo holds 7,900 litres. Murray said he needed more fuel than that to make our next planned stop in Crete which was about five hours away. I told him we would be fine. He sulked off, muttering.

Ron found moisture in a cannon plug connecting the start light to the starter. Apparently the moisture froze at altitude and trapped air which expanded as it warmed on the descent through 5,000 feet. It activated the pressure switch which turned on the light. Ron cleaned it and we were back in business. By now I would have normally been switching pilot/copilot duties on each leg, but Murray wasn't offering and I preferred to stay in the right seat. As copilot, it was easier to manage the fact that, to him, I could do nothing right.

We departed for Iraklion, Crete, late in the day and ran smack into a headwind. Murray was fit to be tied. The GPS showed that we would run out of fuel about the time we got there. I stayed silent while he ranted and then I called Italy control. I obtained a direct routing and a clearance up to 13,000 feet. With the new routing, we would make it. The higher altitude reduced our fuel burn and got rid of the headwind. We had to go on oxygen, but that made it harder for Murray to yell at us. We landed at Iraklion with a full two hours fuel remaining.

The flight did not pacify Murray at all. Our fuel and accommodation arrangements at Iraklion were in place, but as soon as we arrived at the hotel, Murray asked if our overflight clearances for Africa had arrived. They had not. It was late and we were all tired. Murray exploded into his worst foul-mouthed tirade yet. I went to bed.

The overflight clearances were at the front desk in the morning along with confirmation of arrangements to pick up a spare engine in Cairo, Egypt. This was news to Charlie. He didn't know anything about a spare engine. It had been arranged by the leasing company which was providing the airplane and Clarkin, not World Wide Aircraft Ferrying. Stopping at Cairo did not fit the refuelling arrangements which had them overflying Cairo and landing at Luxor. To refuel at Cairo and skip Luxor wouldn't work since the Buffalo would not fly non-stop to their destination, Lokichokio, Kenya. South of Luxor, they would be overflying Sudan where civil war precluded stopping. Now it was Charlie's turn to question the arrangements, but he didn't.

We flew a three-hour leg to Cairo the next morning. No one on the amp at the Cairo Airport knew anything about the arrangements to load the engine. Murray exploded again. I knew the Egyptians and I knew that yelling at them would not get anything loaded. I couldn't listen to him anymore. I'd managed about ten hours sleep in the last 60 hours. I told Murray that I was going to a hotel to sleep and if he ever got the engine loaded he could call me. I left him to fend for himself and went to bed.

I slept right through to the middle of the night. Murray called me about 3 o'clock in the morning to say that the engine was loaded. He wanted to depart before dawn to make up for some of the lost time. He was surly but calmer. I told him I would be there shortly.

When I arrived at the airport, everything had been done except the loaders hadn't been paid. They wanted $1,500, cash, which was more than I had. I had to borrow $700 from Murray which made him angry again. I paid and we left.

We hadn't refuelled in Cairo so we flew an hour and a half to our planned stop in Luxor. There we had confirmation of prepaid fuel through World Fuel Services.

When we landed, we were met by the refuellers. The foreman said there was no prepaid fuel for us. "Pay cash," he said in broken English, holding out his hand, "must pay cash."

Murray launched into another tantrum. I couldn't really blame him this time, but I was tired of listening to him. We knew the fuel had been prepaid, but it was obvious to me that losing your temper wasn't going to help. I didn't want to pay either. We were running out of cash and I suspected the refueller was trying to scam us for a double payment of the fuel, but we didn't have enough to go somewhere else.

I told Murray to go inside to clear customs and file our next flight plan. When he had left, I told the foreman to go to the office and look it up, "World Fuel Service," I said.

He wouldn't budge. "Pay cash," he replied.

I motioned him to come into the airplane with me. When we were out of sight of the rest of the ramp crew, I showed him a roll of American money that I kept in my pocket to speed things along at stops such as Egypt. It was mostly one dollar bills, but I had put a ten around the outside to make it look like more money than it was.

"This is yours," I said, holding out the roll, "you fill up on World Fuel Service."

He reached for the money, but I held onto it. "Fill up on World Fuel Service. I will go with you to the office."

"No," he said loudly, "you stay here." He climbed down and headed for the office. In five minutes, he came out and directed the refuellers to go ahead. When they were done, he brought me a form to sign that was made out to World Fuel Service with our registration already on it. I gave him the roll of money.

We departed Luxor and flew the length of the Nile River to where the south end of Sudan borders Kenya.

Lokichokio was a military base in Kenya but the United Nations used it to service Kenya, Sudan and Ethiopia. The runway was compacted gravel. The coordinates were available in the African Jeppesen book so we were able to fly right to it without any problem. It was in a military defense zone. Jeppesen outlined complicated arrival procedures which required us to fly a corridor and call in at regular check points. The base was defended by Kenyan fighter jets and anti-aircraft guns. We must have complied with the procedures correctly. No one fired at us. Our plan was to off load the camp equipment then fly on to Nairobi where the engine was to be changed. I was to fly home from Nairobi on the airlines. Murray's attitude greatly improved as soon as we arrived at Loki. He politely asked me if I would stay a couple of days in the camp while they got everything squared away. I agreed and was given my own tent.

The camp was quite comfortable. While I was there, I was invited to go to one of the nearby villages with one of the natives. It was like stepping back 2,000 years. The village was a living National Geographic article. The people were dirt poor and leading a very primitive existence. Their houses were straw-roofed huts and they scratched out a living tending a few scrawny goats and domesticated antelope. The women wore stacks of beads around their necks to press their shoulders down. The rings were their most valuable possessions. The biggest problem in the area was a lack of clean water. The goats drank the sewage draining from the United Nations compound.

Charlie met the young Australian who was going to be Clarkin's copilot. He had an opportunity to talk to him when Clarkin was not around.

He was obviously on his first job flying a large, multi-engine turbine. I told him that Murray was a good pilot but a hard man.

"Bite your tongue as long as you can and you will get ahead building hours in this airplane. Whatever you do for Murray, it won't be right, so just get used to it."

I stayed three days in Loki before flying to Nairobi. We had to borrow some of the UN fuel which we pumped from 45-gallon drums.

Murray had to promise to load up with replacement fuel in Nairobi.

Murray was pleasant enough during the two hour flight but I was glad to see the last of him and be headed for home.

CHAPTER THIRTY-SIX

June, 1996
Through Russia with money

"The enforced stop cost us $1,000 U.S. and we didn't buy any fuel."

Mark Harper

𝕸ichael Bannock called me from World Wide Aircraft Ferry and asked if I would deliver two Hawker Siddeley 748s from New Zealand to Whitehorse, Yukon. I said "Yes" almost immediately. I knew that the end of the cold war had opened Russia to civilian aircraft. It was a chance to fly a new route.

Michael didn't have a copilot lined up. I needed someone under 60 years old who was endorsed on the 748 to satisfy the New Zealand authorities. Michael faxed me a resume from a 29-year-old pilot that he thought was qualified. Mark Harper was a Newfoundlander who had been flying HS 748s for Air St. Pierre. This is the airline that operates from the French islands of St. Pierre and Miquelon off the coast of Newfoundland. Mark's resume indicated that he had international experience flying in Angola. I called him up. He seemed to know 748s very well and sounded like the right kind of guy. I hired him on the telephone and never regretted it.

Charlie met 29-year-old Mark Harper in Toronto on June 4. Together they flew on Air Canada to Los Angeles and then Air New Zealand on a 14-hour leg to Sidney, Australia, followed by a two and a half hour leg to Christchurch, the largest city in New Zealand's South Island.

There, they saw the airplanes they were to deliver; two HS 748s sold to Air North in Whitehorse by Mount Cook Airlines based in Christchurch. They would take one now and the other one in a couple of weeks.

In Christchurch we met Tom "Ace" Wood, a mechanic and part owner of Air North. He had checked the airplanes over. Both 748s were at least 30 years old. The first one had 50,000 hours on it, but was obviously well maintained. It was equipped with a full complement of navigation radios including a modern HF. Mark and I had both brought portable GPS receivers, so the only thing we had to do before departing was clamp our GPSs to the glare shield over the instrument panel and take off.

We flew a short shakedown leg to Auckland, New Zealand, on top of the North Island. This gave Mark and I a chance work out our crew coordination and to check the aircraft's fuel consumption before launching over the ocean. Officially, Mark was the captain to satisfy New Zealand authorities, but we traded seats and jobs on each leg of the delivery.

Their next destination was Norfolk Island, Australia, a speck in the ocean 500 nautical miles northwest of New Zealand. Norfolk had originally been a penal colony but had turned into a resort destination. Charlie and Mark stopped there just long enough to refuel and have the sale of the aircraft transacted. This saved Air North some taxes.

From Norfolk Island, the two pilots flew to Brisbane, Queensland, mid-way up the east coast of Australia for fuel and an overnight stopover.

About three quarters the way across the Tasman Sea, the left generator failure light illuminated. I was flying as captain at the time. I tried recycling the generator, but couldn't get it to come back. This didn't pose an immediate problem. The weather was good but it was dark by the time we reached the Australian coast. If the other generator had failed, we would have eventually lost all electrical power. The generator on the other side continued to work fine. It carried the electrical load we needed, but we knew that we had to get the problem fixed before heading further north.

The following day we were able to get a Pacific Airlines mechanic to troubleshoot the problem. He discovered that the generator control unit had failed. We were carrying boxes of spare parts for 748s and the list indicated that we had two GCUs on board. Mark and I searched every box and couldn't find either one. I called Mount Cook Airlines in Christchurch and talked to Ace Wood. He told me that they had pulled out the box containing the two GCUs with the intention of splitting them up, one for each airplane, but they had mistakenly left both sitting on the hangar floor. He could have sent one of them by courier, but it was a Friday and the following Monday was a holiday in Australia. An overnight delivery service could not get it to us before Tuesday. To speed things up, Ace agreed to take the airlines to Brisbane the next day with the GCU in his hand luggage.

Mark and I spent the rest of the day doing a little sightseeing around Brisbane. We visited the old Expo site where I had delivered the Partenavia to the Italian Pavilion in 1988.

Ace arrived mid-Saturday and we spent the rest of the day helping him change the GCU. We ran the engine up and the generator worked. We were in business again.

Ace had originally planned to fly back to Whitehorse from Christchurch on the airlines. He asked if he could fly with us instead. This is against World Wide Aircraft Ferrying policy because of problems with pushy aircraft owners in the past. I told him that he could come with us as long as he understood that if he interfered with our operation I would tell him to go and sit in the back. He promised to be no trouble.

We departed early on Sunday morning northwestward for Mount Isa on the other side of Queensland. This is the headquarters for Australia's Flying Doctor service in the centre of the arid cattle land. We refuelled and flew to Darwin, on top of Australia's Northern Territory for an overnight stop.

Ace was as good as his word. He didn't interfere and was a fun guy to be with. It helped to know that we had a mechanic on board the aircraft.

The next day we flew north to Manado in the central islands of Indonesia just north of the equator. Skyplan International was to take care of our refuelling arrangements, handling and overflight clearances. We got fuelling and handling at Manado but no Indonesian overflight clearance. They wouldn't let us go. Mark and I spent two hours getting nowhere with the officials in the airport office until an Indonesian Air Force general took pity on us. He arranged our overflight clearance in a few minutes.

From Manado, we flew the length of the Philippines to Manila. Here we were supposed to have handling. The lady who was hired to do it didn't show up. We found out later that Skyplan had given her the wrong day because they were working from the other side of the International Dateline. I bluffed my way through the customs and airport procedures as if we had handling. The officials either didn't notice or didn't care. Mark was impressed. He commented that the airport officials automatically looked to me. "I'm supposed to be the captain, but everyone knows by your age that you're in charge."

The following day we flew across the South China Sea to Okinawa, south of Japan. Skyplan had corrected our handling dates, so everything was arranged when we arrived. We had to delay our departure from there so that we wouldn't arrive at our next stop, Sappora on Japan's north island of Hokkaido, too early. We had a slot time reservation and couldn't miss it either way.

I have never seen ramp service like there was at Sappora. There must have been half a dozen ramp workers, all in uniforms and all wearing gloves. Clearing customs, the fuelling, the ride to the hotel, everything was handled superbly.

We got to sleep in the next day because our slot time for departing that morning was late. The delayed departure left us with time for just one leg that day, from Sappora to Petropavlovsk in Russia. Petropavlovsk is on the long Kamchatka Peninsula that separates the Sea of Okhotsk and the Bering Sea.

When we switched to Russian control, the altitudes had to be given in metres and the altimeter settings were in millibars. The IFR clearances contained altitudes and headings, but no limit. Nothing was left up to the pilot's discretion. We were expected to follow the controllers' instructions. Their English was very limited to the basic phrases of IFR instructions. Any deviation from that did not compute with them. This was particularly scary on the approach to the Petropavlovsk Airport. The weather was overcast and required some flight in cloud. We were never cleared for the approach. We were given headings and altitudes to fly but they did not conform to the Jeppesen approach charts that we had. We found the airport okay, but the terrain on that peninsula is rugged. Any mistake in communications could have been fatal.

It only took us five hours to fly from Japan to Russia, but it was a huge leap back in terms of economics and culture. Petropavlovsk was an important Russian Air and Naval Base. What we saw made it obvious that the end of the cold war had been hard on it. The airport contained a large inventory of parked military aircraft that looked like they would never fly again. The runways were part paved and part gravel. The airport staff were dressed poorly. The women didn't wear any make-up. Nobody smiled. The ground crew asked us if we had any ear plugs on the aircraft to give them. We did not.

We were met by a French Canadian handler who spoke Russian. He arranged for our refuelling, customs clearance and a ride to the hotel. Everything had to be paid in roubles which we got from the handler. The vehicle to the hotel was a 1930s design. The accommodation was very basic and the hotel menu was limited. I ordered fish and beer on the theory that it was a seaport and that beer is pretty safe anywhere else in the world. Mark had the beef and regretted it through most of the night.

The next morning we tried to file a flight plan to Nome, Alaska. The airport officials would not accept it. We were told that we had to stop again in Russia to "export" ourselves. There was no reason for this except to give the Russians a chance to extract more fees. We filed for Provedeniya across the Bering Sea from Nome.

We took off and flew northeast along the rugged Russian coast. Again, we were not flying to a clearance limit like you do in the rest of the world, but continued from one set of instructions to another. We had gone most of the way when we were told to land at Anadyr, the last airport before Provedeniya. We didn't want to land there. We didn't need fuel and the weather was not particularly good. We were flying on top of cloud and didn't relish another Russian-style vectored approach. The controller wouldn't hear of it any other way. We had no choice.

We shot the approach and landed without difficulty. It was June, but it was still cold and windy. We were hoping to just pay the airport fees and then get out of there. Mark went into the terminal building and Ace and I stayed with the aircraft. In a few minutes, a customs officer came out to the aircraft. We greeted him cordially, communicating in nods, gestures and smiles. He sat down in the airplane and made himself at home. Since we weren't speaking the same language, we soon ran out of things to say. Ace had a bottle of rum in his bag, so he pulled it out and offered the man a drink. This was obviously a universal language in Anadyr. I left them to it. By the time Mark came back two hours later, both Ace and the customs officer were well and truly drunk. The Russian had removed all of his uniform badges and pins and given them to Ace as a gesture of goodwill. Mark reported that the enforced stop cost us $1,000 U.S. and we didn't buy any fuel. At least we didn't have any trouble with customs. We helped the Russian off the airplane stripped of all rank and external identification and then beat a hasty start and taxi.

It was late afternoon by the time we were airborne again, but the June sun in that part of the world never really sets. When we landed at Provedeniya, the tower controller told us that the airport was closing. He asked us if we needed fuel, food and accommodation. We answered "Yes" to all three. He was very helpful. He arranged for the fueller to stay late and had the airport kitchen reopened just for us. Apparently, there was no other restaurant in the town near the airport.

The controller came down from the tower and acted as a translator for us. We were only allowed to pay in roubles and we didn't have any. The airport officials could not accept dollars or credit cards. There were no bank machines. The controller said he would round up roubles for us in the morning and we could pay then. He loaned us enough money to buy supper and to pay for the hotel.

We met a Russian pilot, copilot, navigator and stewardess from an Antonov 24. They had arrived ahead of us on a commuter run up the coast. The navigator spoke a little English. He said that the captain was interested in seeing the inside of our airplane. We welcomed him on board. He was very excited about the equipment that we had in the cockpit. I found this a little strange considering the 748 was a 30-year-old airplane. His airplane was closed up for the night, but the navigator said we could see it in the morning.

The only thing on the menu at the restaurant was borscht and wieners. We rode into town with the airport staff in a rickety old bus that must have been built in the 1930s. At the hotel, we asked for three rooms. Through gestures and nods, we were made to understand that accommodation was scarce. We were given the "President" suite to share together. It was filthy. The bedding had obviously been used many times.

We walked around town looking for more food. The shops were still open but their shelves were mostly bare. We managed to buy half a loaf of bread and six bottles of beer.

Back at the hotel, we invited the Russian airline crew to join us for bread and beer. They readily agreed. The captain brought a smoked salmon which we cut up with my pen knife. Mostly we talked about flying, but it was a time for elections in the newly independent Russia. They were obviously afraid for its future.

We found most of the Russian people on that trip to be as nice as they were allowed to be. They were never unfriendly, but the country is struggling with huge economic and political problems brought on by its separation from the USSR.

The next morning I counted out $2,700 U.S. for the fees and fuel for the air traffic controller. It was absolutely the last of my cash. He handed me a big box which he said contained nearly 12 million roubles. I said that I didn't have time to count it. He laughed and said that the airport officials would make sure that it was enough to cover our bills.

We thought we were done until the customs officer asked to see our Russian visitor visas. None of us had one. Visas were not required for flight crews passing through other countries, but we weren't going anywhere as far as the customs guy was concerned. I thought if a country did require a visitor's visa, you would be kicked out if you didn't have one. Not in Russia. It took several phone calls to Moscow and a lot of wasted time before the officials in Provedenyia Bay decided they had permission to let us go.

We met the airline crew and were given a tour of their Antonov 24. It was primitive even by HS 748 standards. The passenger seats were military style tube and canvas. When I saw the cockpit, I understood the captain's excitement over our equipment. There were two flat, console-mounted compasses like the ones used by allied bomber crews in World War II. The radar had a hooded scope like the ones found in our military interceptors in the 1950s.

We finally got airborne and pointed the airplane across the Bering Strait to Alaska. It was just before noon, but that high up on the globe it soon became late afternoon. We crossed the international dateline and seven time zones during our five hour flight to Whitehorse.

When we flew into American airspace the controller didn't recognize the New Zealand aircraft registration. He asked where we were from. "New Zealand," I replied.

"Welcome to America," he said. "You don't know how glad we are to be here."

Our arrival at the Air North base triggered a celebration. Purchasing the two 748s was a big deal for the small company. The airplanes were being used to replace Douglas DC 3s, Air North's largest aircraft up to then. Mark and I stayed overnight and joined the festivities. It was good to see people smiling.

The following day, we took the airlines to Vancouver. I stayed there one more night before heading home to rest up for the next Air North delivery through Russia.

CHAPTER THIRTY-SEVEN

July, 1996
Through Russia with perfume

"The gesture nearly brought her to tears."
Charlie Vaughn

When Charlie returned home between his two flights through Russia, he went shopping. His first stop was the industrial safety supply store in St. Catharines. He asked for a large bag of ear plugs. The store owner thought he knew all of his bulk ear plug customers. He asked Charlie what they were for. Charlie told him about his flight through Russia including a mention of the linecrew's lack of hearing protection. To emphasize the story, Charlie showed the man a Russian 100,000 rouble bill. He told him it was worth about $20. The man was intrigued enough to ask Charlie if he would exchange the Russia note for the ear plugs.

I knew I would be seeing boxes of those bills on our next trip. I readily agreed.

Charlie's next stop was the local tourist bureau where a description of his Russian trip netted him bags of pins from the city, the region and the province.

In Russia, exchanging pins was popular as an international gesture of friendship. I was well stocked to be the friendliest visiting pilot on my next trip.

Lastly, Charlie contacted the local Mary Kay and Amway representatives. He wanted to buy a quantity of small sizes from their cosmetic and perfume collections. When they heard that he planned to distribute them through Russia, they donated large bags of samples.

On four days rest and with slightly enlarged luggage, Charlie and Mark Harper repeated their marathon airline travel from Toronto to New Zealand. They arrived in Christchurch on June 25 to pick up the second Hawker Siddeley 748 for Air North.

We met Joe Sparling in Christchurch. Joe was a pilot and the principal owner of Air North. Ace Wood had told him so much about the previous trip, that Joe asked if he could come along on this one. I agreed under the same "no interference" conditions as I had given Ace. Mark liked the idea of having him along since the young Newfoundlander would be out of work when our delivery was finished.

"Nothing like using a flight half way around the world for a job interview," he said.

Joe turned out to be a super guy. He helped with everything from making lunches in the galley to flying the airplane.

The 748 on this trip was the oldest of the two, but still in good shape. It had a fixed crystal HF transmitter, so we installed a portable HF with selectable frequencies. I had brought it with me on the first trip, but had not used it. That was all we needed to get ready. On June 26 we departed Christchurch. We had more confidence this time, so we bypassed the shakedown leg to Auckland and flew directly to Norfolk Island and then on to Brisbane, Australia.

Over the next two days, we followed the same route north as the last trip to Mount Isa, Darwin, Indonesia and on to Manila, Philippines. Skyplan messed up our dates again. They had us arriving in Manila a day later than we did. This was no problem except they were unable to move up our landing slot in Sapporo, Japan. We had to spend a day and two nights in Manila letting our schedule catch up to us. This was not as frustrating as it sounds. The long trips are a lot easier if you can kill some of the jet lag with a day of rest, which is what we did. We also did some sightseeing around

Manila. The city is incredibly crowded and polluted, but it's crowded with some of the friendliest people in the world.

We departed Manila for Okinawa and then on to another white glove ramp reception in Sapporo.

On July 1, we flew to Petropavlovsk. On that leg, Mark handled the radio communications. He received the usual Russian point-to-point IFR clearances with their specific altitudes and position report requirements. We were unable to make contact on one call due to atmospheric interference on the HF, so we simply continued to the next point and called there.

After we landed, Mark was grilled by the air traffic control supervisor. He wanted to know where we had been when we were out of contact. Mark told him that we continued enroute. This would have been obvious to anyone bothering to calculate time, speed and distance, but the man had it in his head that we had somehow accelerated to an incredible speed to spy on Russia's secrets. His menacing tone was loud and clear through his thick English accent, but he eventually let us go.

Our handler, pre-arranged by Skyplan, was a pretty Russian girl. Her English was excellent and she was very helpful. She exchanged our money for roubles and arranged for fuel and hotel. She explained away the bad attitude of the air traffic controller with a Russian expression that she translated into, "the dog must bark".

I gave the linecrew a bag of ear plugs and some pins. We distributed pins around to the other workers in the terminal building. Mark even gave the control supervisor some pins. I thanked our handler and gave her a bag of cosmetic and perfume samples and some pins. The gesture nearly brought her to tears.

"But I have nothing to give you," she protested.

"You have given us your good service," I said.

"But it is so much," she replied.

I told her to share them with her friends.

The next morning, she met us at the airport with a small collection of gifts including a book about Boris Yeltsin, a

Russian doll key chain and some pins. She was wearing make-up.

"My friends thank you very much," she said.

Our gifts to the Russians bore immediate fruit. We were allowed to file a flight plan all the way to Nome, Alaska. In the air, we were not forced to land anywhere along the route. This saved us lots of time and money. My only regret was that it prevented us from meeting more Russian friends and distributing more gifts. It was fun to see the smiles in the drab surroundings.

From Nome, we flew to Whitehorse. Mark and I stayed there two days to help Air North properly celebrate the arrival of their 748s. When we left, Joe Sparling promised Mark that he would call him about a job when the 748s had been added to their operating certificate. He earned it.

CHAPTER THIRTY-EIGHT

November, 1996
Don't call me a legend

"Legends are things from the past. I'm not finished yet."
Charlie Vaughn

This book started out as the story of Charlie Vaughn's aviation career. It is incomplete. After three years of interviews, Charlie and I agreed to cut it off. In the fall of 1996, Charlie turned 70-years-old. He had been flying for 50 years. It was time to stop interviewing and to publish a book.

There are aviators and episodes important to Charlie that are not mentioned. The book does not describe the hundreds of student pilots that Charlie helped into aviation during the 1950s and '60s. It is missing Charlie's stint as a captain flying on Canada's shortest airline route from St. Catharines to Toronto with Air Niagara in the early 1970s. The search for St. Catharines businessman Hugh McFarlane who went missing in his float equipped Cessna 185 on a stormy weekend has not been covered. Nor have the many hours spent flying Newman Brother's Cherokee Six, TSM. We didn't cover Charlie's introduction to corporate jets as a cross-anada courier pilot for Air Niagara in a Citation 500. "They told me I could qualify as a captain after a minimum of 100 hours as a copilot. At the end of the first week, I had 20 hours. One of the captains quit and suddenly I was qualified."

There is no mention of the fifteen years Charlie spent flying as a part-time copilot on Dupont's different Westwind executive jets out of Toronto airport. We missed Charlie's three trips around the world in seven weeks delivering Fairchild Metros from Canada to New Zealand. We didn't cover the trips with Bill Bolton and Norm Bailey to Khartoum in war-torn Sudan to try and bring out an HS 748. There was another 748 delivery to Sri Lanka from Manchester, England, with Cam Mclean. There was an interesting story about Charlie finishing the delivery of a Buffalo when a crew from the Zambian Air Force abandoned it at St. John's, Newfoundland.

We missed Charlie's second trip with Joe Deluce, this time in a Fokker F-28 from Toronto to Papua New Guinea. We also didn't cover the sightseeing flights over Niagara Falls that Charlie is still doing for Niagara Air Tours out of St. Catharines in a Cessna 206. "I really enjoy those. The passengers are on holiday from all over the world. They are friendly and interesting."

The people associated with these stories shouldn't take their omission personally. Charlie and I just ran out of time before he ran out of stories.

Perhaps Charlie's most significant statement after having flown all over the world is that it has made him appreciate Canada. "There is no better place than here," Charlie claims. "The other countries and cultures are interesting but seeing them makes me realize how lucky we are in Canada."

The people he has met are more important to Charlie than the places. "The people around the globe are great. I think the news media make the world seem worse than it is. I have never been in a situation where there hasn't been a person there willing to help me."

"I now have aviation friends everywhere. In Canada, whenever I get on an airliner, I try to visit the cockpit. I either know one of the pilots or at least we have a mutual acquaintance."

When we were searching for a title for this book, I suggested to Charlie that he had reached legend status in aviation. This bothered him.

"Legends are things from the past," he retorted. "I'm not finished yet. Don't call me a legend."

Okay, Charlie.

Garth Wallace